Christmas Cookbook

Christmas
Cookbook

A HOLIDAY
COOKBOOK

by
Susan Purdy

FRANKLIN WATTS / NEW YORK / LONDON / 1976

This is a birthday book for Muffin
and
un cadeau rose pour Charley, Katia, *et* Marleni

For help in the development and testing of these recipes, I am indebted to many people. I am especially grateful to Sara Jane Chelminski for sharing her culinary wisdom and giving constructive advice during many hours in our testing kitchen. I would also like to thank Michael and Valeska Chelminski; my sister, Nancy G. Lieberman; Bea Joslin; Katia and Marlene Kanas; Maria Peterdi; Tracy, Julie, and Pat Glaves; Elizabeth MacDonald; Rachel Chodorov; Joan Sommer; Norma Bredbury; Marianne Swan; Mary Katsiaficas; Jeannie Stone; Diane Walins; Barbara Cover; and the late Anna Olson. For inspiring my appreciation of creative cooking, as well as for practical artistic help, I thank my mother, Frances Joslin Gold. The most colorful bouquets of all go to my husband and daughter, Geoffrey and Cassandra, for their loving and patient support, thoughtful advice, and marathon cookie-eating.

Library of Congress Cataloging in Publication Data

Purdy, Susan Gold, 1939–
    Christmas cookbook.

    (A Holiday cookbook)
    Includes index.
    SUMMARY: Recipes from around the world to celebrate Christmas, Epiphany, New Year's Day, and St. Lucia's Day.
    1. Christmas cookery—Juvenile literature. [1. Christmas cookery] I. Title.
TX739.P8   641.5′68   76–24884
ISBN 0–531–01207–7
ISBN 0–531–02373–7 pbk.

Contents

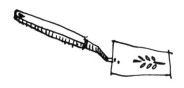

Before You Begin

If the arrangement of these recipes looks different to you, it is. I have told you what foods to get ready in case you are going shopping, then listed ingredients and instructions when and where you actually use them. My testers find this method easy to use; I hope you will agree. I also hope *you* will have the patience to read all the way through a recipe before starting it. This will help you plan your time as well as your activities.

With the help of this book, I hope you will discover the fun of creative cooking as well as the pride of accomplishment when you make something others enjoy.

1. Safety: Keep pot handles turned away from the stove front so pots will not be bumped into and spilled. Turn off oven or stove-top as soon as you are through using it. To prevent fires, keep potholders, dishtowels, aprons, and your clothes away from stove burners. Keep a fire extinguisher in the kitchen just in case (and learn how to use it).

To prevent accidental cuts, store and wash knives separately from other utensils.

2. Butter: All butter used for the recipes in this book is lightly salted unless otherwise noted, when it will say "sweet, unsalted." Margarine can almost always be substituted for butter, and in many recipes both are listed. In recipes that taste much better made with butter, margarine has been left off the ingredients list.

3. Flour: For better nutrition, use *unbleached* all-purpose flour instead of bleached. You will find the word *unbleached* on the front of the flour package.

4. Health-food substitutions: To increase nutritional value of recipes, you can substitute 1 to 2 tablespoons of sifted soy flour or sifted noninstant powdered milk for an equal amount of flour in cookie and cake recipes. NOTE: Soy flour causes quicker browning, so if you use it, lower temperature about 25°. Wheat germ has already been added to many recipes; 2 to 3 tablespoons more can be added to most baked goods if you like. Turbinado (unrefined) sugar can be substituted for an equal amount of granulated white sugar. To substitute honey for granulated sugar, use about ⅞ as much (1 cup sugar = ⅞ cup honey) *and* use about 3 tablespoons *less* liquid in recipe.

5. The timer: Whenever a recipe gives two times (such as 10 to 12 minutes), set your timer for the first time (10). Test for doneness. If necessary, reset timer for additional time (2 minutes) and cook longer.

6. Oven heat: Oven temperatures vary. It is very rare for the actual temperature inside the oven to be exactly the same as the one you set on the thermostat dial. If your foods do not cook in the time or manner described in the recipe, it may be because your oven is too hot, or not as hot as the heat indicated by your thermostat. To be safe, use a separate oven thermometer (sold in a hardware store) that hangs or sits on the oven shelf. Change the temperature on your outside thermostat dial until the inside oven temperature is correct.

7. Cleanliness: Whenever you are cooking, it is a good idea to wash your hands first and put on an apron. When you will actually be handling the ingredients in a recipe (as in shaping dough) a special hand-washing note is added to the recipe.

8. Cleanup: To keep other members of your family happy about your kitchen adventures, clean up when you are finished. To make this almost painless, fill up the sink with warm soapy water when you start to cook. Add dirty pots or spoons as they accumulate. Then they are soaked and ready to be washed (or go into the dishwasher) when you are through cooking. Put ingredients away as soon as you are finished with them. Mop up spills as they occur.

Measurements

All measurements in this book are level. Thus, "a cup of flour" means that the cup is filled and then the top is leveled off with the blade of a knife (see Basic Skills). Here are some useful measurements:

1 pinch = less than ⅛ teaspoon	12 tablespoons = ¾ cup
= the amount you can	16 tablespoons = 1 cup
pick up between your	= 8 ounces
thumb and forefinger	2 cups = 1 pint
3 level teaspoons = 1 level tablespoon	2 pints = 1 quart
4 tablespoons = ¼ cup	4 quarts = 1 gallon
5⅓ tablespoons = ⅓ cup	8 ounces = ½ pound
8 tablespoons = ½ cup	16 ounces = 1 pound

METRIC SYSTEM

In the United States we measure both liquids and solids by volume. The metric system also measures liquids by volume, in milliliters (ml) and liters (l), but dry ingredients are measured by weight, in grams (g) and kilograms (kg). Thus, to convert dry ingredients into their metric equivalents, you must know their weight in ounces (oz.) or pounds (lbs.). When you know the customary measurement for dry ingredients:

Dry	Multiply by	To Find
ounces	28	grams
pounds	0.45	kilograms

When you know the customary measurement for liquid ingredients:

Fluid	Multiply by	To Find
ounces	30	milliliters
pints	0.47	liters

Then round off the figure to the nearest usable measure.

Here are some examples (all quantities are rounded off):

1 cup 10X confectioners' sugar, unsifted = 4 oz. = 110 g
1 cup granulated white sugar, unsifted = 7 oz. = 200 g
1 cup unbleached all-purpose flour, unsifted = 4½ oz. = 125 g
1 tablespoon salt = ½ oz. = 15 g
1 teaspoon salt = $^1/_6$ oz. = 5 g
1 cup butter = 8 oz. = 225 g
1 cup milk = 8 oz. = 250 ml
1 tablespoon milk = ½ oz. = 15 ml
1 teaspoon milk = $^1/_6$ oz. = 5 ml

Basic Skills

To Level Measurements:

All measurements in this book are level unless otherwise specified. To level a measuring cup or spoon, fill it until slightly mounded, then draw the back of a knife blade over the top, scraping the surface flat. Don't pack down the ingredients.

To Measure Butter or Shortening:

Butter or margarine is easiest to measure when purchased in quarter-pound sticks.

1 pound = 4 sticks = 2 cups
1 stick = ½ cup   = 8 tablespoons

Instead of measuring by the stick, you can pack the butter down very firmly into a measuring cup (be sure there are no air spaces trapped in the bottom), or you can use the "water displacement" method: To measure ¼ cup butter, fill a 1-cup measuring cup ¾ full with water. Add pieces of butter until water reaches the 1-cup mark. Pour off water and you are left with ¼ cup measured butter.

To Sift Flour:

Sifting lightens the texture of baked goods. You can use either a strainer or a sifter for this process.

Sift the specified amount of flour onto a sheet of wax paper. Then pick up paper, pull the edges around into a sort of funnel, and *gently* pour as much flour as you need back into a measuring cup. You can also use a spoon to transfer flour. Do not shake or pack measured flour. Level top of cup with knife, then add flour to recipe. Or return re-measured flour to sifter, add other dry ingredients, such as baking powder and salt, and sift everything together into other ingredients in recipe.

To Add Eggs to Recipe:

You may notice that whenever an egg is to be added to a bowl full of ingredients, it is first broken into a cup. That is so you can pick out the shells—should any accidentally fall in—before the egg disappears under the waves of flour or sugar in the bowl. I avoid asking you to add any "whole eggs" because I did that once in a cooking class and guess what happened? Right! Shell and all—just as requested.

To Separate an Egg:

Here are two different ways to separate an egg. The first method may be new to you, but try it anyway. It is very easy, never breaks the yolk, and is a lot of fun.

First wash your hands, as you will be touching the egg. Crack egg in half by tapping it sharply against side of bowl. Hold egg on its side as shown, grasping ends with your fingers. Fit tips of thumbs into crack. Pull shells apart and *at the same time* turn one half-shell upright so it contains all the egg. Hold this shell, containing egg, upright with one hand while the other hand discards the empty half-shell. Then turn empty hand palm up, fingers together, over a clean dry bowl. Pour out the entire egg onto the fingers of the empty hand. Spread fingers apart very slightly to let the egg white drip between them into the bowl while yolk rests on top of the fingers as shown. Collect all of the white in a bowl; put yolk in separate bowl.

The most common procedure is to break egg in half, then hold half-shell containing the yolk upright in one hand while you pour the egg white from other half-shell into a bowl. Then tip yolk out into the empty shell while white that surrounds it falls into bowl below. Place yolk in separate bowl.

To Roll Out Dough:

There are two ways to roll out dough. One is on a countertop or a pastry board, the other between sheets of wax paper. If you are using a countertop or a pastry board, spread it lightly with flour so the dough will not stick. Also flour the rolling pin. Then roll out the dough, adding more flour if dough sticks. Some pastry boards and rolling pins are covered with a cotton cloth (called a sock) to help prevent sticking; cloths should also be floured.

The second method is to cut two pieces of wax paper, each roughly 14″ long. Place one piece flat on the counter and flour it lightly. Place dough on floured paper, then sprinkle a little flour on top of dough. Cover dough with second paper. Use rolling pin (unfloured) to roll out dough between the papers. Peel the paper off and put back on again if it gets too wrinkled. When dough is correct thickness, peel top paper off dough.

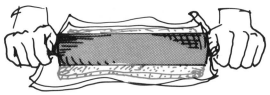

To Use a Garlic Press:

A whole garlic is made up of a cluster of separate cloves, each wrapped in its own thin skin. The easiest way to peel the skin off a clove of garlic is to set the clove on a wooden board or counter and smack it hard with the bottom of the garlic press. This breaks the skin so you can pick it off easily with your fingers.

To press the garlic, open the jaws of the garlic press. Set peeled clove inside, then press handles together, forcing garlic out through the holes into the bowl below. Use a spoon or knife to scrape off any pieces of garlic that cling on the outside of the holes. Discard the dry fibers left inside the press. NOTE: If you don't have a press, finely chop the peeled garlic with a sharp knife.

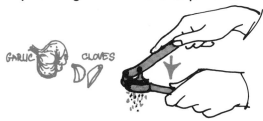

To Chop an Onion:

"Chopping" with this method means you actually cut the onion into dice, or small pieces. First, peel the onion. Then cut the onion in half lengthwise, from root to stem (a). Place one half cut-side down on board. Hold it with fingers gripping sides, root end to the left (if you are right-handed). Slice onion as shown (b), with point of knife facing root end. Cut almost, but not all the way through root end; this will help hold onion together. Finally, make narrow cuts in the opposite direction (c), cutting across the first slices to produce the "chopped" or diced pieces. Keep moving your fingers back away from the knife.

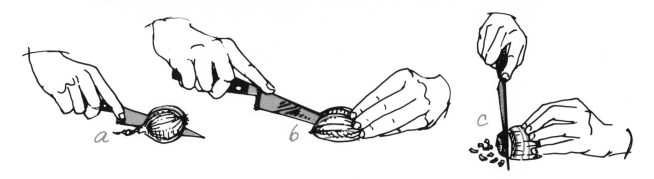

To Measure Temperature of Candy Syrup:

If you do not have a candy thermometer, follow directions below to determine syrup temperatures. Boil sugar syrup following recipe directions. When ready to test temperature, remove pan from heat so it will not overcook. Spoon a drop of syrup into a glass of ice water. Syrup should form a ball. Pick the ball out of the water with your fingers. SOFT-BALL STAGE (234°–240°): Ball should hold together, but be soft and pliable. HARD-BALL STAGE (250°–268°): Ball should feel firm between your fingers.

If your test drop is too runny to form a ball, or if the ball is too soft, return pan to heat, cook syrup 1 or 2 minutes longer, and test again. Syrup can take a while to get near the right temperature, but once it does, the heat can suddenly shoot up over the mark. So beware, and test often. NOTE: Soak pan in hot water to remove hardened syrup.

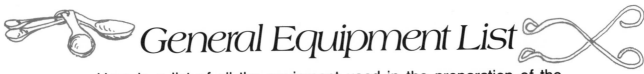

General Equipment List

Here is a list of all the equipment used in the preparation of the recipes. Each recipe will require the use of only a few items. This list is included only as a guide; if you do not have the exact utensil specified, substitute whatever you think will work.

We have measured pots and pans to their *outside* edges, then noted how much water they hold when filled right to the very top. A round pan is measured across its center (the diameter). To see if your own pot is the same size, or nearly so, fill it up with carefully measured cups of water.

Teacup
Measuring cups
Measuring spoons
Wooden spoon
Slotted or large spoon
Table knife, fork, teaspoon,
    butter knife (dull blade)
Long-handled fork
Tongs
Paring knife
Kitchen knife
Bread knife
Scissors, kitchen shears
Rubber scraper
Spatula
Pancake turner
Eggbeater
Wire whisk
Electric mixer
Colander
Sifter
Strainer
Rolling pin
Pastry board (optional)

Cookie cutters (*or* drinking
    glass turned upside down)
Pastry brush
Wire rack
Cake tester *or* toothpicks
Potato ricer *or* potato masher
Vegetable peeler
Grater
Garlic press
Nut grinder (optional)
Blender (optional)
Lemon squeezer *or* juicer
Candy thermometer (optional)
Oven thermometer (optional;
    see Before You Begin,
    step 5)
Timer
Airtight container (such as
    plastic freezer box with lid or
    metal tin with lid)
Serving platter *or* tray
Paper *or* plastic bag
Potholders
Hotpad *or* trivet

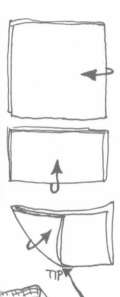

Decorating tube (You can make your own by cutting a piece of wax paper about 12″ × 18″. Bring the short ends together to fold it in half, then in half again. Roll paper into a cone, with the tip along the folded edge as shown. Tape cone to hold it and cut off tip to make small hole. Fill with frosting, fold ends over, and squeeze down until frosting is forced out hole in tip.)

Double boiler

Ring mold *or* tube pan (9″ diameter holds 6 cups water)

Soup bowl (holds about 2 cups water)

Mixing bowls: small (holds about 4 cups water); medium (8 to 10 cups); large (14 to 16 cups—this wide-topped bowl is used for mixing batters and doughs)

Saucepans: small (holds about 4 cups water); medium (8 cups); large (11 to 12 cups)

Large pot *or* Dutch oven (holds about 20 to 24 cups water)

Electric skillet

Frying pans: small (about 6″ diameter); medium (8″ to 9″ diameter); large (10″ to 12″ diameter)

Bread pans (Dimensions of these plans will vary widely; as long as your pan is *approximately* the size specified, the recipe will be successful.): large loaf (9¼″ × 5¼″ × 2¾″—holds 8 cups water); average loaf (9″ × 5″ × 2¾″ *or* 9″ × 5″ × 3″—holds 8 cups water); medium loaf (8″ × 4¼″ × 2¼″—holds 4 cups water); baby loaf (6″ × 3½″ × 2″—holds 2 cups water)

Cookie sheets (Flat, or with narrow edge. Cookies are easier to remove from a flat sheet. Shiny sheets bake and brown most evenly. Cookie sheet should not cover the entire oven shelf or it will block circulation of heat. For best results, use a sheet that allows at least 1½″ of shelf space around all edges. To bake, place sheet on middle shelf of oven.): small (13½″ × 10″); large (average—17″ × 14″)

Jelly roll pan (15½″ × 10½″ × 1″)

Christmas Trimmings to Make and Eat

MOLDED SUGAR BELLS

If you ever made sand castles at the beach, you are already an expert on the art of bell-making. Damp sugar is packed into a bell-shaped cup just the way sand is packed into a beach pail. Then it is turned over, unmolded, and left to dry in the air. Nothing could be easier, and the finished bells make unique—and edible—decorations. You can hang them on your Christmas tree or use them to trim your party table.

NOTE: One recipe makes about 12 bells, but they are made in batches of 4 or 5 at a time. Each batch needs 2½ to 3 hours to dry on the outside. Then the damp sugar is spooned from inside the bells and remolded into new bells. To make all 12 bells, plan to begin this project in the morning and come back to it at intervals during the day. Molded bells can also be left on wax paper overnight (see step 10). Decorate the bells or patch any cracks with Royal Icing (see index).

EQUIPMENT:
Bell mold—a wine goblet, juice glass,
   or teacup with bell shape (flared rim
   and rounded base, as shown)
Tray—large enough to hold 12 bells
Wax paper
Large mixing bowl
Teacup
Measuring cups and spoons
Large mixing spoon and teaspoon
Round wood *or* plastic toothpick *or*
   darning needle
¼" wide ribbon (or wool)—30" length for
   hanging up each bell
Jingle bells—½" diameter tin bells with
   hanging loops sold in five-and-ten-
   cent stores
Scissors

FOODS YOU WILL NEED:
3½ cups granulated sugar
1 egg white
¼ teaspoon vegetable food coloring *or*
   beet juice (for red color)

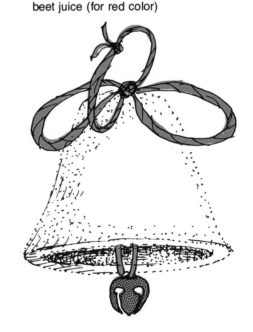

Ingredients:	**How To:**
(To make about 12 bells 2¾" wide at rim and 2½" high. Bells can, however, be any size you like. Double recipe to make more bells.)	1. Select your mold. Set it beside the tray. Cover tray with a piece of wax paper.

3½ cups granulated sugar
1 egg white

2. Measure sugar into bowl. Separate egg (see Basic Skills) and add egg white to sugar in bowl. Place yolk in a teacup and set it aside for some other use.

¼ teaspoon vegetable food coloring (optional—the juice from canned *or* freshly boiled beets should be used instead of red food coloring to make pink bells)

3. Sugar can be left white for plain bells, which can be trimmed with brightly colored ribbons. Or, you can color sugar by adding about 25 to 30 drops (¼ teaspoon) of food coloring *or* beet juice. If you do not color sugar, add the same number of drops of water to moisten it.

4. Use spoon to mix together all ingredients in bowl. If you have added coloring, it should be mixed in evenly.

5. Wash your hands. Then squeeze sugar mixture in your hands. If sugar is damp enough, the impression of your fingers should be clear. If it is not, add a few more *drops* of water and mix.

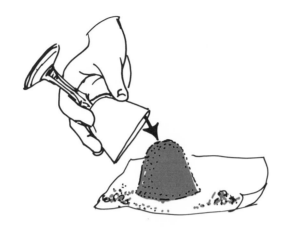

NOTE: If sugar sticks in cup, it is too wet; return it to bowl and add more dry sugar. If bell crumbles when unmolded, sugar is too dry; return sugar to bowl and add a drop or two more water. After a little practice, molding bells will be very easy (just like molding sand castles).

6. Pack sugar firmly into mold.

7. Turn mold upside down over paper-covered tray. Tap side or bottom of mold gently but firmly with your hands, or give the edge of the rim a tap on the tray. A neatly formed sugar bell should drop gently onto paper as you lift mold off. If bell looks uneven, pat it back into shape with your finger.

8. Repeat step 7 until all prepared sugar is used up. Depending on mold size, you will probably be able to mold 4 *or* 5 wine goblet bells *or* 3 teacup bells.

9. Leave bells to dry on paper for about 2½ to 3 hours (longer in damp weather). Large bells may take longer. The longer bells dry, the thicker their sides will be.

10. After drying, bells should feel firm and dry on the outside. Pick one up *gently* and turn it upside down. You will see that the sugar in the center is still damp. Cradle bell in one hand and slowly and carefully scoop the damp sugar out with the teaspoon. Place damp sugar

back in bowl. Leave bell walls about ¼″ thick. Set scooped-out bells down on their *sides* to complete drying of inside walls. (If bell crumbles from handling, return it to bowl, dampen sugar with a few drops of water, and remold bell. Let other bells dry longer.) NOTE: Bells *can* be left standing on wax paper overnight before being hollowed out. In the morning the sugar inside will still be damp, but the sides will be thicker than if hollowed out after only 3 hours.

11. With toothpick or darning needle, make a small ribbon hole in the rounded end of each completed bell. Then widen hole to be about ¼″ × ⅛″ as shown.

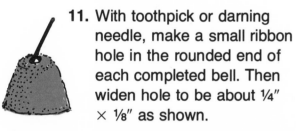

12. Attach ribbons and jingle bells (if you want them) as follows. Cut a 30″ length of ribbon. String bell on, placing it at ribbon center. About 2″ above bell, tie both halves of ribbon together in overhand knot as shown. Then tie a second and third knot on top of the first to make it fat enough not to slip through hole.

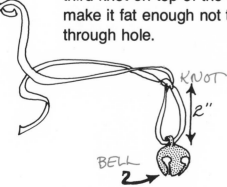

13. Fit both ribbon ends up inside bell and poke them out of hole in bell's top. Use toothpick to help push ribbons out. *Be gentle* so sugar does not crack. (Don't forget, cracks can be patched with icing colored to match bell.) Pull ribbons up slowly until knot rests against inside of bell top.

14. Tie ribbon ends into a bow. Tie bow loops together into a double knot. Then tie loose ends together into a hanging loop. Hang finished bell on your Christmas tree. Store bells wrapped in tissue paper in a large airtight tin or cardboard carton.

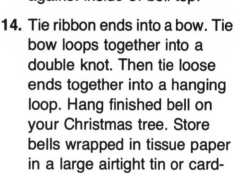

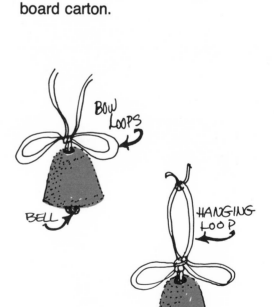

MAPLE SYRUP POPCORN BALLS

This recipe is made with maple syrup, but you will find that it tastes remarkably like Cracker Jacks and is just as hard to resist nibbling! Large popcorn balls are fun to make, but you can also form small 1″ balls—or irregular lumps of the coated popcorn—to make bite-sized candies. Or fit small balls on top of ice-cream cones, and tie them with ribbons to hang on the Christmas tree.

EQUIPMENT:
Measuring spoons and cups
2-quart saucepan
Candy thermometer (optional)
1 or 2 wooden spoons, 1 large serving
   spoon
Drinking glass
Large mixing bowl
Wax paper
Rubber scraper
Paring knife *or* kitchen scissors
Plastic wrap *or* colored cellophane
Ribbon *or* wire twisters

FOODS YOU WILL NEED:
2 cups maple syrup
Water
1 or 2 ice cubes
10 cups prepopped corn
¼ cup wheat germ
½ cup chopped nuts *and/or* gumdrops
2 tablespoons butter *or* margarine
1 teaspoon vanilla extract

Ingredients:

(To make 10 balls 2½″ in diameter)

2 cups maple syrup

How To:

1. Since you will form the popcorn balls with your hands, be sure to wash your hands before starting recipe.

2. Measure syrup into saucepan. If you have a candy thermometer, clip it onto the side of the pan. It should be on a slant so the tip does not rest directly on the bottom of the pan.

Glass of water containing 1 or 2 ice cubes

10 cups popped corn (sold in grocery stores; or pop your own following directions on corn package)

¼ cup wheat germ

½ cup chopped nuts (any type) *and/or* ½ cup cut-up gumdrops

3. Place saucepan over medium heat. Bring syrup to a full boil—when lots of bubbles start to rise up in the pan. Immediately turn heat down a little, so syrup continues to boil but the bubbles appear more slowly. Stir gently every now and then with wooden spoon.

4. Boil slowly until candy thermometer reads 260°, or until a drop of syrup turns into a hard ball (see Basic Skills) when spooned into a glass of ice water. Grade A pure maple syrup will take about 40 to 45 minutes to reach this point. The time will vary depending on your type of syrup.

5. While syrup is cooking, measure popcorn into large mixing bowl. Add wheat germ and nuts *and/or* gumdrops, which you have cut up with a knife or kitchen scissors. Toss all together with 2 big spoons.

6. Alongside bowl, set out a piece of wax paper for drying balls.

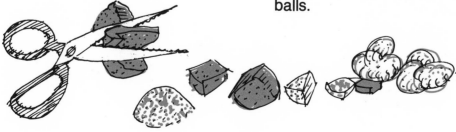

2 tablespoons butter *or* margarine

1 teaspoon vanilla extract

7. When syrup is ready, remove it from the heat. Stir in butter *or* margarine. Slowly stir in vanilla, taking care that mixture does not "spit" as the cool liquid touches it. Stir well.

8. Pour hot syrup over popcorn mixture in bowl; use rubber scraper to remove all syrup from pan. Toss and turn mixture with 2 large spoons until all pieces are well coated.

9. While syrup on popcorn is still warm (but *not* too hot to touch) use your hands to mold the popcorn into balls of whatever size you like. Don't let mixture get completely cold, or you will not be able to mold it. Set balls on wax paper. Or just pull apart the coated popcorn and set the uneven lumps on the wax paper to harden. If mixture feels too sticky, butter your hands as you work.

10. When popcorn balls or pieces are hard—in 15 or 20 minutes—wrap them in squares of plastic wrap or cellophane. Fasten with ribbon or a wire twister. If you make a loop of ribbon, you can hang the balls on the tree. They will stay fresh several weeks.

STAND-UP COOKIE TREE

You can use this tree for a centerpiece, then eat it for dessert.

EQUIPMENT:
Same as for Rolled Sugar Cookies (see
    index), *plus*:
Paring knife
Masking tape
Tracing or typewriter paper
Pencil
Scissors

FOODS YOU WILL NEED:
Same as for Rolled Sugar Cookies (see
    index)

TREE STANDING UP

How To:

1. Follow recipe for Rolled Sugar Cookies, steps 1 to 5, and place dough in refrigerator to chill. Do *not* grease cookie sheets.

2. To make a pattern, set your tracing or typewriter paper over the tree pattern page in this book. Tape edges of paper to a table. Use pencil to trace around the outside and inside lines on tree. Untape paper. Cut out the paper around the *outside* lines of the tree.

3. Divide dough into 3 balls of equal size. Use 2 balls to make the tree halves and save the third for decorations or regular cookies.

4. Roll out 1 dough ball between 2 floured sheets of wax paper (see Basic Skills). Roll dough into a rectangle roughly 7½″ × 8½″ and ⅜″ to ¼″ thick. Peel off top layer of wax paper.

5. Flour pattern lightly, then set it down on rolled dough. Cut around outside edges of tree with tip of paring knife. Then, with tip of knife, draw around (but don't cut through) the outline of the *striped* area in the lower half of tree. Peel off pattern. Cut out striped slot as shown.

SLOT

WAX PAPER

TREE PATTERN

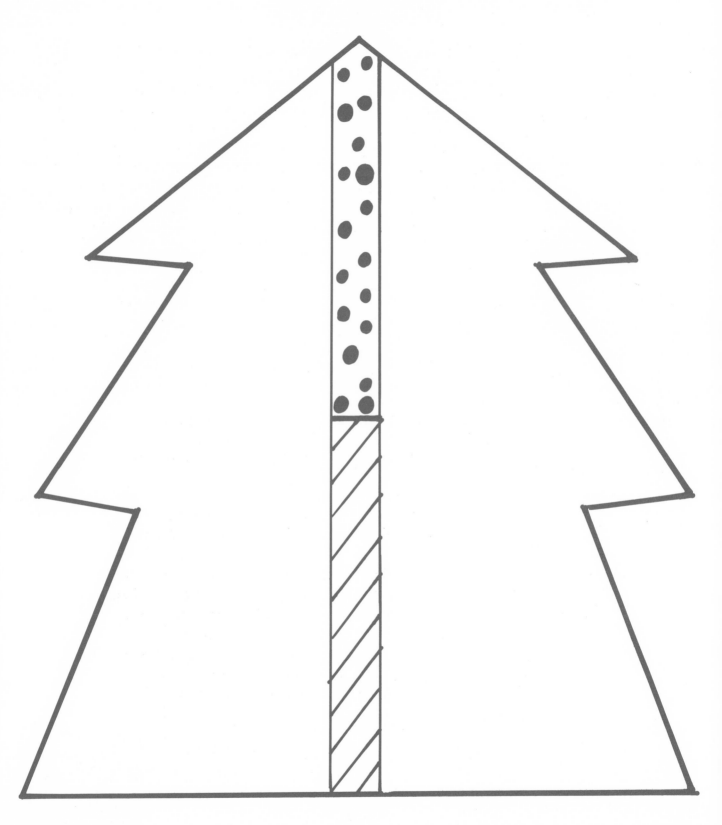

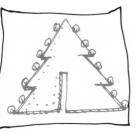

6. If you wish, you can now decorate outer branches of tree by pressing on small balls or narrow ribbons of scrap dough. Touch a drop of water to the spot before adding dough to make it stick. Do *not* add decorations along midline or at peak of tree. Dough decorations may be omitted if you prefer.

7. Excess wax paper should be cut away, so only about 2″ extends around tree. Lift paper with the tree on it and set it on ungreased cookie sheet. (Paper will not burn in oven.) With knife blade, straighten out edges of cut tree slot to be sure sides are a full ½″ apart.

8. Place cookie sheet in the 350° oven. Set timer for 10 to 11 minutes, and bake tree until it is lightly golden around the edges. Use potholders to remove cookie sheet from oven. Let tree stay flat on pan until cold (about 15 minutes).

9. While the first tree is baking, roll out the second dough ball as you did the first (step 4). Set pattern on top of dough and cut around outside edges with tip

of knife. Then draw around the lines of the *dotted* area in the upper half of the tree. Peel off pattern. Cut out dotted slot as shown. Decorate this tree if you did the first, following step 6. Cut away excess wax paper and bake second tree as you did the first, steps 7 and 8.

10. Trees can be put together as soon as they are cold, or while still flat on paper, they can be trimmed with Royal Icing (see index) tinted with vegetable food coloring. Do *not* put icing on peak or along midline of either tree. When icing on one side is dry and hard, turn trees over and decorate their backs. When icing is completely hard, assemble tree as follows.

11. To make tree stand up, fit the slot of one into the slot of the other as shown. Do not force them or press down too hard, or the cookies will break. If the slots are wide enough, they should fit very easily. (If any pieces break, patch cracks with icing.) Stand completed tree on round mirror or flat platter.

Festive Breakfasts

"DRAW YOUR OWN" WHEAT-GERM PANCAKES

The addition of yogurt makes these pancakes so light and delicious that they may become your favorite breakfast or lunch treat. At our house, they are a Sunday morning tradition, especially popular when shaped like slightly overblown horses or dogs.

For a Christmas party, you can "draw" your pancakes in the shape of trees, stars, horses, or stick figures by dripping batter—a small amount at a time—from a spoon onto the frying pan.

We recommend making pancakes on an electric skillet right at the table. That way, your guests can share the fun of designing the pancakes and watching them cook, and you do not have to keep jumping up to make more at the stove. Serve pancakes with warmed syrup (which can be flavored with a dash of cinnamon if you like). Pancakes are also good dotted with butter and sprinkled with sugar *or* spread with honey *or* jam.

EQUIPMENT:
2 small saucepans *or* 1 saucepan and 1 small stove-to-table pan with pouring spout (for heating and serving syrup)
Frying pan *or* griddle *or* electric skillet
2 mixing bowls—1 small, 1 medium-sized
Measuring cups and spoons
Eggbeater *or* wire whisk
Large spoon
Rubber scraper
Pancake turner

FOODS YOU WILL NEED:
3 to 3½ tablespoons butter *or* margarine
¾ to 1 cup maple syrup *or* honey *or* jelly *or* jam
1¼ cups all-purpose flour
1 tablespoon baking powder
¼ teaspoon salt
1 tablespoon granulated sugar
2 eggs
⅓ cup yogurt (plain *or* flavored) *or* sour cream
1 cup milk, approximately
⅓ cup wheat germ
½ cup chopped nuts *or* fresh fruit (optional)
Seedless raisins (optional)

STOVE-TO-TABLE PAN

Ingredients:

(To make about 20 pancakes, 4" in diameter)

2 tablespoons butter *or* margarine
¾ to 1 cup maple syrup

1¼ cups all-purpose flour
1 tablespoon baking powder
¼ teaspoon salt
1 tablespoon granulated sugar

2 eggs
⅓ cup yogurt (plain *or* flavored) *or* sour cream
1 cup milk

⅓ cup wheat germ
NOTE: For an added treat you can also add ½ cup of finely chopped nuts *or* peeled, chopped apples *or* finely sliced peaches or nectarines *or* berries *or* sliced bananas

How To:

1. Place butter *or* margarine in small saucepan and set over very low heat until just melted. Place maple syrup in another saucepan or in stove-to-table pan and set to warm over low heat.

2. Turn electric skillet on to 350° or set frying pan or griddle on low heat to start warming.

3. Sift flour, baking powder, salt, and sugar into *small* bowl. (Sifting makes pancakes somewhat lighter in texture, but if you are in a hurry, you can forget it.)

4. Break eggs into medium-sized mixing bowl. Add yogurt *or* sour cream. Beat with egg-beater or whisk until thoroughly blended and creamy. Add milk and beat again.

5. Spoon entire flour mixture—a little at a time—into egg-yogurt-milk mixture. Beat slowly after each addition of flour.

6. Add wheat germ and the butter you have been melting. Use rubber scraper to empty the pan. If you like, stir in any extra ingredients such as nuts *or* fruit.

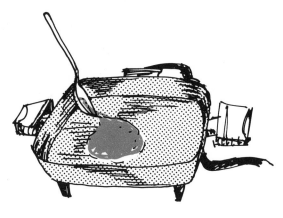

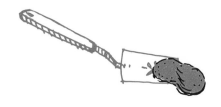

1 to 1½ teaspoons butter *or* margarine

7. Batter should now be the consistency of very heavy cream. It may thicken a little as it sits, so add 1 or more tablespoons milk if it needs thinning at any time.

8. Raise heat to medium-high under frying pan, griddle, *or* electric skillet. Add butter or margarine to coat pan. Lower heat slightly if butter smokes. When butter sizzles, drop 1 large spoonful of batter onto pan, making the first test pancake.

9. Cook pancake about 2 minutes—until bubbles appear on its surface, or until it looks slightly firm around the edges. Turn pancake over with pancake turner. It should look golden brown. Cook on other side about 1½ minutes, or until golden brown. (Watch the pancake, not the clock!)

10. To "draw" pancakes, fill spoon with batter. Hold it over hot pan and dribble out batter in the shape you want. Add more batter if needed. Forms spread when cooked and will look a little fat and lumpy, but recognizable. Add raisin or nut eyes to faces if you like.

    Repeat step 8 to make additional pancakes, but do *not* add more butter to pan between batches.

FRITTATA

This Italian specialty is a sort of pancake-omelet filled with vegetables. It makes a delicious breakfast or brunch dish. Serve it with sausages, juice, and milk or cocoa. A frittata with a green salad will turn any lunch into a party!

EQUIPMENT:
Garlic press
Paring knife
9″ or 10″ frying pan with oven-proof
    handle *or* 9″ baking dish that can go
    on stovetop as well as in oven
Measuring cups and spoons
Wooden spoon
Medium-sized saucepan with lid
Colander (if cooking spinach)
Potholders
Mixing bowl
Eggbeater *or* wire whisk
Broad spatula *or* pancake turner
Trivet *or* heat-proof table pad

FOODS YOU WILL NEED:
2 tablespoons cooking oil
1 clove garlic
½ medium-sized yellow *or* white onion
1 cup fresh *or* frozen spinach leaves *or*
    ½ cup of other filling (see recipe)
¼ cup water
½ teaspoon plus 1 pinch salt
6 eggs
⅛ teaspoon pepper
⅛ teaspoon dried thyme *or* oregano
2 tablespoons grated Parmesan cheese

Ingredients:

(To make 4 servings)

2 tablespoons cooking oil
1 clove garlic

½ medium-sized yellow *or*
   white onion

How To:

1. Measure oil into frying pan *or* baking dish. Press garlic and put into frying pan (see Basic Skills).

2. Chop or "dice" enough onion to make ¼ cup (see Basic Skills).

3. Set pan over low heat and sauté (cook slowly), stirring occasionally with wooden spoon. Onion will turn a light golden color. This will take about 5 minutes. *Then turn off heat.*

1 cup (packed down) fresh *or* frozen spinach leaves *or* ½ cup of any other filling such as sliced raw mushrooms, chopped sweet red or green peppers, chopped cooked ham, sliced fresh tomatoes, or any combination of these ingredients.

¼ cup water

Pinch of salt

6 eggs
½ teaspoon salt
⅛ teaspoon pepper, preferably freshly ground
⅛ teaspoon dried thyme *or* oregano

4. Cook frozen spinach according to directions on package. To prepare *fresh* spinach, first wash front and back of leaves under running water. Shake leaves over sink to remove most water, then place them in saucepan.

5. To cook *fresh* spinach, add water to leaves in saucepan. Cover pan and bring water to boil over medium heat. Boil 1 minute.

6. Turn off stove. Set colander in sink. Hold pan handle with potholder and *carefully* carry pan to sink. Drain frozen or fresh spinach through colander. Sprinkle pinch of salt over spinach.

7. Add cooked and drained spinach (or other filling) to garlic and onion in frying pan.

8. Break eggs into mixing bowl. Add salt, pepper, and thyme *or* oregano. Beat well with eggbeater or whisk.

9. Place frying pan over medium heat. Sauté filling-onion mixture about 2 minutes, stirring with wooden spoon.

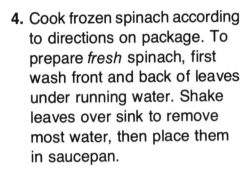

(30)

10. Preheat broiler. Pour eggs over vegetables in frying pan. Cook over medium-low heat. After a *couple* of minutes, eggs will start to become solid. Use spatula to lift eggs around edges of pan. Tip pan slightly so loose eggs can run onto bottom of pan. (Do not mix up or scramble eggs.) When eggs are *almost* solid but still look soft on top, *turn off heat*.

2 tablespoons grated
Parmesan cheese

11. Sprinkle cheese all over top of eggs.

12. Holding pan with potholders, *carefully* place it under broiler. Broil about 3 minutes, or until cheese is lightly browned. Frittata will puff up slightly. Turn off oven.

13. With potholders, carry pan to table and place it on trivet *or* heat-proof pad, Cut frittata into wedges like a pie. Serve with spatula directly from pan.

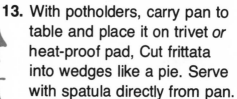

BRAVO!

SANTA LUCIA SAFFRON
BUNS AND BREADS

In Sweden, the Christmas season really begins with the celebration of Lucia Day, the Festival of Light, on December 13. In the early calendar, this date was the shortest day of the year, the happy moment when the worst of winter was over and the days would begin to lengthen into spring. Lucia, whose name means "light," was chosen to be the patron saint of the festival, for she is believed to help hurry away the darkness of winter. One of the most important traditions for this day is the baking of sun-colored Santa Lucia Saffron Buns.

Early on the morning of December 13, the eldest daughter of each family dresses up as Lucia, wearing a white gown with a red sash. On her head she wears an evergreen wreath topped by real candles. Her younger sisters wear the same costume, without the crown. Together, they prepare a tray of coffee (or cocoa) and their saffron buns, baked the day before. Lucia carries the tray and, singing the traditional melody "Santa Lucia," they all parade through the house serving breakfast to the other members of the family.

NOTE: The sunny yellow color and sweet aroma of this recipe come from the use of saffron, the dried stigmas of a special variety of crocus flower. Saffron is sold along with spices in the grocery store, but if you can't find it, substitute yellow food coloring.

This is a good recipe for a group project, with each cook sharing in the mixing, kneading, and shaping of the dough.

EQUIPMENT:

Small soup bowl
Teaspoon
Measuring cups and spoons
Medium-sized saucepan
Potholders
Slotted metal mixing spoon or wooden
  spoon
Wire whisk (optional)
Large round mixing bowl—about 12" in
  diameter, 5" or 6" high
Rubber scraper
Wax paper

Wooden pastry board or marble slab or
  thoroughly washed and dried counter-
  top for kneading dough
Roasting pan or pot (optional)
Timer
2 cookie sheets or 2 loaf pans (9" × 5" ×
  2¾", approximately)
Scissors or paring knife
Ruler or tape measure
Pastry brush—softest type available
Spatula
Wire rack

FOODS YOU WILL NEED:

2 packages (¼ ounce each) active dry yeast *or* 2 small (1-ounce) cakes of compressed yeast
Water
1 cup granulated sugar
1 cup (2 sticks) butter
2 cups milk
Pinch to ½ teaspoon saffron *or* 8 drops yellow food coloring
1 teaspoon salt

2 eggs
About 8 cups (2 to 2½ pounds) all-purpose flour
1 to 1½ tablespoons salad oil (*not* olive oil)
2 or 3 tablespoons butter, margarine, *or* oil—to grease pans
Seedless raisins *and/or* whole *or* ground blanched almonds for trimming
Sweet (salt-free) butter (optional)

Ingredients:

(To make about 24 buns or 2 regular or crown-shaped loaves)

½ cup warm water
2 packages (¼ ounce each) active dry yeast *or* 2 cakes (1 ounce each) compressed yeast, crumbled
1 teaspoon sugar

1 cup (2 sticks) butter
2 cups milk
Saffron—from a large pinch to 1/2 teaspoon, depending on how much you have, *or* substitute about 8 drops yellow food coloring
1 teaspoon salt
1 cup—minus 1 teaspoon—sugar

How To:

1. Run water from tap until it feels comfortably warm—*but not hot*—against the inside of your wrist (as if testing a baby's bottle). Measure warm water into small soup bowl. Sprinkle both packages, *or* cakes, of yeast over the water. Add 1 teaspoon sugar, stir with spoon, and set bowl aside while yeast dissolves. NOTE: Yeast is a living organism. Water that is too hot will kill the yeast and keep bread from rising.

2. Add butter to saucepan and set it over low heat until *just* melted. Then hold pan steady and pour in measured milk. Leave pan on low heat until milk is warm, *not hot*. Then turn off heat. Remove pan from stove. Crumble saffron into pan *or* add food coloring. Add salt and sugar. Set pan aside to cool slightly.

SAFFRON

1 egg

3. Break egg into mixing bowl. Beat egg with spoon *or* whisk. Then test temperature of butter and milk mixture. If it feels comfortably warm to your (*clean*) finger, but is *not* hot, pour it over the egg, beating as liquid is added.

4. Have a look at your bowl of dissolved yeast. It should smell sweet to you. You should see, and even hear, it bubbling slightly as it starts to make the gas bubbles that will raise your dough. Use the rubber scraper to add dissolved yeast to egg-milk mixture in large bowl. Blend together.

5 cups all-purpose flour

5. Measure about 5 cups flour— 1 cup at a time—into liquid in large mixing bowl. Beat with spoon or whisk after each addition of flour. Continue beating until batter is well blended and begins to stretch.

Mixing now is important, for it helps develop the "gluten" in the flour. Gluten is the part of the wheat that combines with the gas from the yeast to make the dough rise.

2½ to 3 cups all-purpose flour

¼ cup—or more—flour

FOLD

PUSH

TURN

6. Add 2½ to 3 cups more flour, stirring with spoon until dough feels too stiff to mix. (Every once in a while, use spoon to scrape dough down from sides of bowl.) Dough should start to hold together in a ball, but it will still be somewhat sticky to the touch. NOTE: The amount of flour you need will depend upon several things, including the type of flour and the humidity of the weather.

7. Wash your hands. Sprinkle about ¼ cup flour over pastry board, marble slab, *or* counter. Turn bowl on its side and spoon dough out onto floured surface. Set bowl in sink and fill it with hot water to soak, so you can wash it for later use.

8. Sprinkle flour on your dry hands. Knead dough by folding it over toward you, then pushing it away while leaning on it with the heels of your hands. Give dough a quarter-turn and repeat the folding and pushing. The flour from the board will soon work itself into the dough. If dough still feels sticky, add more flour—1 tablespoon at a time—and continue kneading. All together, kneading will take between 5 and 10 minutes. (If you find it easier, knead ½ or ⅓ of the dough at a time.)

9. Kneading is complete when surface of dough looks and feels quite smooth. It should not be sticky. You may see bubbles stretched across, or under, the skin of the dough. Set dough aside to rest. You may even want to rest yourself, after all that kneading.

10. Wash and dry mixing bowl. Then grease inside with 1½ tablespoons oil. Place ball of dough in bowl and turn it over and around so its surface is covered with oil. (This will prevent a hard dry crust from forming on the rising dough.) Cover bowl with lightly oiled piece of wax paper.

11. The dough is now set aside to rise. In order for the yeast to work properly, it must be in a warm place (70° to 80°), away from cold drafts. Your rising place must be a protected corner of the counter in a warm corner of your kitchen, or the back of your stove-top, or a rack inside your oven (with the heat *off!*). If you choose the oven (and this is the spot I prefer for the first rising), place a roasting pan or pot of hot water on the oven floor to keep the temperature evenly warm.

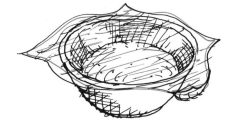

12. Check the clock or set the timer for 1½ hours. It will take between 1½ and 2 hours for the dough to puff up and double in size. NOTE: If you must unexpectedly leave dough during this stage, place covered bowl in refrigerator to slow down the rising. Dough can even be refrigerated overnight if necessary, with a plate over the bowl. The next day let chilled dough warm through completely before counting rising time. Rising may take longer if you do this, but the quality will not be affected.

13. After about 1 to 1½ hours, check the dough. To tell if it has risen enough, first see if it looks about twice as big as it was. Then poke two fingers down into the dough. If the holes stay, dough has risen enough; if dough springs back, let it rise a little longer. If you used a pan of water in the oven, remove it now.

POKE!

14. Wash your hands. Now *punch!* your fist right down into the center of the dough. There are two reasons for doing this: first, it is so much fun, and second, your punch knocks some of the extra air bubbles out of the dough.

PUNCH!

15. Remove dough from bowl and set it down on *lightly* floured work surface (see step 7). Knead dough a couple of times to remove more air.

16. Generously grease cookie sheets *or* loaf pans with butter *or* margarine *or* oil. Set pans aside.

17. Lightly flour your clean, dry hands, then shape dough into buns or loaves as follows. Place shaped buns at least 2″ apart on greased sheets. Buns rise again before baking, so they will need space in which to grow. NOTE: See shapes on next page.

Lucia Crown Buns (1 recipe makes about 24): Pull off a lump of dough about 2″ in diameter. Roll it between your palms to make a ball, then press to flatten it slightly. Set dough on floured board. Shape it into a crescent about 3½″ to 4″ long. With scissors *or* knife, make about four ½″-long cuts in top curved edge. Set bun on greased sheet.

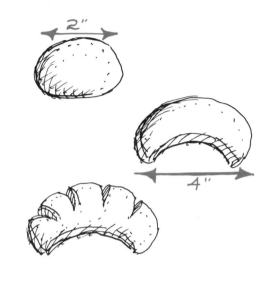

Sun Buns (1 recipe makes about 24): Pull off a lump of dough about 2″ in diameter. Roll it between palms of your hands into a round ball and set it on greased sheet. If you want to make "rays" of sun, use scissors *or* knife to cut about five ½″-inch long cuts all around outside edge of ball.

SUN FACE: SHAPE SMALL BITS OF DOUGH AND PRESS THEM ONTO FLATTENED BALL.

Braided Buns (1 recipe makes about 8 braided buns): When baked, they are actually more like baby loaves of bread about 7″ to 8″ long. Pull off 3 lumps of dough, each about 2″ in diameter. Roll each piece into a rope about ¾″ × 7″. Set the 3 ropes side by side and pinch them together at one

PINCH

Braided Buns (continued):
end. Tuck under pinched ends. Hold this end with the heel of one hand while braiding the lengths together with the fingers of both hands. Turn over each rope and pull it very slightly as you braid it; this will keep it even. When braid is complete (about 5″ to 6″ long), pinch ends together and tuck pinched ends under loaf. Set braid on greased sheet.

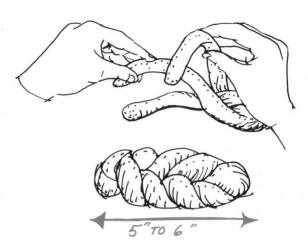

5″ TO 6″

Braided Crowns (1 recipe makes 2 large braided crowns): Divide entire ball of dough in half. Divide each half into 3 equal balls. To make 1 crown, roll each of 3 balls into a rope about 1″ in diameter by 20″ long. Place ropes side by side and braid as for buns, described above. Pinch ends of *braid* together, then pull ends around and join them to form a ring. Pinch ends of *ring* to hold (you may also have to weave in ends to get ring to hold). Set ring in center of greased cookie sheet. Put your fingers inside ring and push sides out gently to form an even circle about 8″ across, measuring to the outside edges.

Regular Loaves (1 recipe makes 2 large loaves): Divide entire ball of dough in half. Pat each half into a rough rectangle, then fold the long edges over onto the surface facing you and pinch them together. Fold over short ends and pinch as shown. Turn dough over, pat gently into oblong shape, and set seam down in greased loaf pan. Ends of dough should be touching ends of pan.

8″

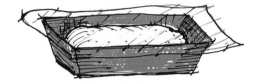

SHAPED   RISEN

1 egg
Seedless raisins *and/or* whole *or* ground blanched almonds *and/or* granulated sugar

18. Cover shaped buns or loaves with lightly greased sheets of wax paper. Set them in a warm place to rise a second time, as in step 11, *except*, do *not* place dough in your *baking* oven, as it must be preheated.

19. Let shaped dough rise until *almost* double in size (about 1½ hours). Don't let dough rise too much this time or it will collapse when it hits the heat of the oven. (If this should happen, your bread will be quite dense and heavy, but still edible.)

20. While dough is rising, use fork or whisk to beat egg in large measuring cup or mixing bowl. Set it aside, along with pastry brush and whatever trimming ingredients you wish: seedless raisins, nuts, *or* sugar.

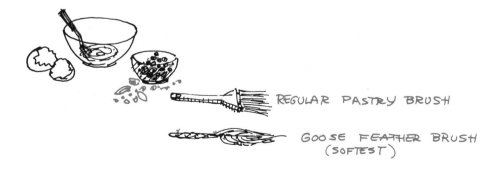

REGULAR PASTRY BRUSH

GOOSE FEATHER BRUSH (SOFTEST)

21. After dough has been rising about 1¼ hours, turn baking oven on to 350°.

22. Watch shaped dough carefully and remove it from rising location as soon as it looks ready. Then dip pastry brush in egg and brush it *lightly* over the top of each bun or loaf. To trim, set 1 raisin *or* whole almond in the center of each cut section on crown-shaped buns, among the twists of a braid, or in the center of a "sun." Sprinkle ground almonds *and/or* sugar over the top of dough.

23. Immediately place dough in preheated oven to bake. Set timer: 25 to 30 minutes for buns, or 40 to 55 minutes for loaves. Test after earliest time. When done, they should be a rich golden-brown color. Use potholders to remove pans from the oven.

24. Put pans on heat-proof surface. Use spatula to remove buns or crowns from sheets. Tip regular loaves from pan. Cool on wire rack.

Buns or loaves should sound hollow when tapped on the top and on the bottom surfaces with your knuckle. If they do not sound hollow, or if they do not feel crisp on the bottom, return them to oven for a few minutes longer.

25. Dough will slice most easily after a few hours, but there is really no good reason to wait that long, especially when it smells so good. Go on, give in . . . and we bet Lucia Day will come more than once a year in your house from now on!

26. Serve buns or bread with sweet butter, as in Sweden. To freeze, cool bread thoroughly, then wrap in airtight plastic bags.

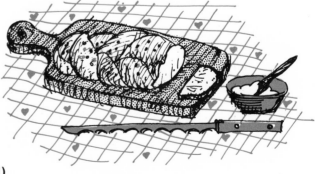

Vegetables and Salads

PEAS IN TOMATO SHELLS

It is much easier than pie to scoop out a tomato and stuff it with peas. These bright red and green vegetables taste as special as they look, decorating each plate at your Christmas dinner. Serve them with any meat dish and rice or potatoes. Or, for a party lunch, serve each guest a plate containing a stuffed tomato surrounded by quartered pieces of a grilled cheese sandwich.

EQUIPMENT:
Oven-proof baking dish
Paring knife
Teaspoon
Mixing bowl
Wire rack *or* wax paper
Medium-sized saucepan with lid
Measuring cups and spoons
Timer
Potholders
Pancake turner *or* wide spoon

FOODS YOU WILL NEED:
Several tablespoons butter *or* margarine
4 medium-sized whole tomatoes
Salt
½ cup water
2 cups fresh or frozen peas (one 10-ounce box, frozen)

Ingredients:

How To:

(To make 4 servings—plan on 1 whole tomato for each serving)

1 tablespoon butter *or* margarine

4 medium-sized whole tomatoes (should be firm and not overripe)

Salt

1. Turn on oven to 350°. Spread butter *or* margarine over bottom of oven-proof baking dish and set it aside.

2. Wash tomatoes. Cut a slice off top of each one as shown. Use spoon to scoop out pulp into bowl. Leave skins about ¼″ thick so they won't fall apart or split when heated.

3. Sprinkle a pinch of salt inside each tomato, then turn it

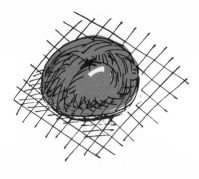

½ cup water
2 cups fresh *or* frozen peas
    (1 10-ounce box)
Pinch of salt

Butter *or* margarine

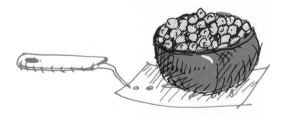

upside down on rack or wax paper and leave to drain while you cook peas.

4. To cook peas, see directions for Rice Wreath (see index), step 15. Drain cooked peas through colander. Sprinkle pinch of salt over peas.

5. Set tomatoes open side up on your buttered dish. Then spoon peas into each tomato shell. Mound peas slightly on top. Put about a ½-teaspoon-sized piece of butter *or* margarine on top of each mound of peas. Save any leftover peas to serve separately.

6. Set dish of stuffed tomatoes in 350° oven. Set timer for 12 to 15 minutes. (The riper the tomato, the less time it should bake.) Then turn off oven.

7. Use potholders to remove dish from oven. Serve tomatoes by lifting them up from the bottom with pancake turner *or* wide spoon. Be careful not to break the shells. NOTE: Sometimes the warm tomato shells do split, but don't worry about it, they will taste just as good.

(43)

SCANDINAVIAN YULE RED CABBAGE

Red cabbage is a traditional part of Christmas dinner in Scandinavian countries, where it is usually served with roast goose. It is a good companion for any roast meat, but also goes well with Fried Chicken and Rice Wreath (see index). This recipe is very easy to prepare and can be made in an electric skillet as well as in a frying pan on the stove.

EQUIPMENT:
Knife
Cutting board
Measuring cup and spoons
Electric skillet with lid *or* frying pan
    with lid
Wooden spoon
Vegetable peeler
Potholders

FOODS YOU WILL NEED:
1 medium-sized head red cabbage
    (*or* two 24-ounce jars ready-made
    red cabbage)
2 tablespoons butter
¼ cup water
¼ cup vinegar (preferably wine
    vinegar)
1 apple
3 tablespoons red currant jelly
½ to 1 teaspoon salt
1 tablespoon caraway seeds (optional)
    or ¼ cup seedless raisins (optional)

Ingredients:

(To make 8 to 10 servings, ½ cup each).

1 medium-sized (1½ to 2 pounds) head red cabbage (NOTE: You can also use 2 large [24-ounce] jars of ready-made red cabbage; heat and flavor as in steps 3 through 8.)

How To:

1. To prepare cabbage, peel off and throw away the 2 or 3 toughest outer leaves. Set cabbage on cutting board and *carefully* cut it in half with knife, then in quarters, like an apple.

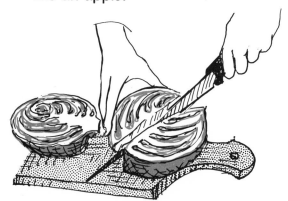

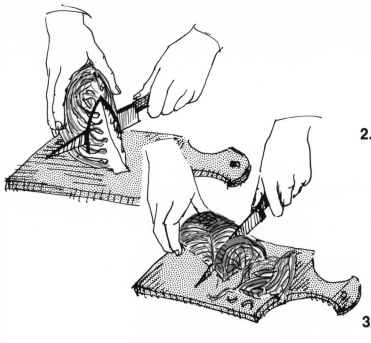

2 tablespoons butter

¼ cup water
¼ cup vinegar

1 apple

3 heaping tablespoons red
currant jelly
½ to 1 teaspoon salt—to
taste
1 tablespoon caraway seeds
(optional) or ¼ cup seed-
less raisins (optional)

2. Cut away the thick white core of each quarter, as shown. Then hold the leaves of each quarter together firmly while you slice them about ⅛″ thick. To avoid cutting your fingertips, be careful to move them back a little farther after each slice.

3. Place butter in skillet or frying pan over 250° (medium-low) heat.

4. When butter melts, add cabbage. Add water and vinegar.

5. Cover pan and cook over medium-low heat about 15 to 20 minutes. Stir now and then with wooden spoon.

6. While cabbage is cooking, peel apple. Place it on cutting board and cut it into quarters. Cut the core off each piece, then cut remaining apple into thin slices.

7. When cabbage is cooked, add apple slices, currant jelly, salt, and caraway seeds (if you like them) or raisins. Gently stir the mixture a couple of times.

8. Heat about 2 minutes more, uncovered, then serve.

SANTA CLAUS EGGS

For a decorative addition to your Christmas breakfast or lunch table, serve each guest a hard-boiled egg Santa on a lettuce leaf. Or put out the trimmings and let everyone join in the fun of creating his or her own Santa.

EQUIPMENT:
Saucepan
Potholder
Small sharp paring knife
Wax paper *or* plate
Teaspoon
Toothpicks (optional)
Paper towels

FOODS YOU WILL NEED:
Eggs—½ egg for each serving,
  plus 1 for trimming
Whole fresh tomato (1 medium-
  sized tomato will make 4 or
  5 Santa hats and noses)
Whole cloves, 2 for each ½ egg
Lettuce leaves

Ingredients:

(Plan on ½ egg for each serving. In addition, make 1 extra egg to use for trimming)

Eggs—at room temperature
  (or warmed for a few
  minutes in a bowl of
  warm water)

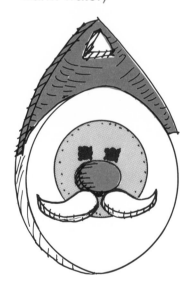

How To:

1. First, hard-boil as many eggs as you will need. To do this, gently place whole eggs in saucepan. Add cold water until it reaches about 1″ above top of eggs. Set pan over medium heat and bring water to a boil. Lower heat slightly and cook at gentle boil for required time—15 minutes for medium to large eggs, 12 minutes for small eggs.

2. When done, turn off stove. Hold handle of pan with potholder and *carefully* carry pan to the sink. Run cold water

(46)

into the pan until eggs feel cool enough to touch. Remove eggs from pan and set them aside to cool 20 to 30 minutes. Or refrigerate them overnight if you want to do this step ahead of time.

3. When ready to trim cold eggs, tap and roll their shells gently on the table. Then peel them. If eggs are still warm, they can be peeled more easily while held under cold running water.

4. Cut peeled eggs in half lengthwise and set them yolk up on wax paper *or* plate.

5. Remove yolk from the 1 extra egg and slice its white into sections about ¼″ to ⅜″ thick. From these slices, cut halves of Santa's mustache, as shown. Each half is about ¾″ long. Also cut small triangles about ¼″ on each side for the tip of each hat.

6. To make Santa's hat and nose, prepare tomato. Wash it and cut it in half. With spoon, carefully scoop out all pulp onto wax paper and save for some other purpose. Leave ⅛″ to ¼″ of outer skin intact. For hat, cut a triangle of this skin about 1½″ on each side. For nose, cut a ⅜″ × ⅜″ oval.

7. To attach Santa's hat, make ½″-deep slit in the widest end of each egg about ¼″ below cut surface, as shown. Fit tomato triangle inside slit with its skin side facing down. Hat will curve upward slightly. Or use toothpick to attach hat to egg just above yolk. Place an egg-white triangle on tip of hat, as shown.

8. Yolk of egg is Santa's face. Press in 2 cloves to form the eyes. (Don't eat the cloves.) Below them set the nose and mustache.

Potatoes, Rice, and Pasta

STUFFED POTATO BOATS

This dressed-up version of the baked potato is easy to prepare and is especially good served with Fried Chicken (plain or Continental style) and a vegetable.

EQUIPMENT:
Paper towels *or* dish towel
Fork
Timer
Potholder
Small saucepan
Measuring spoons
Grater (optional)
Paring knife
Wax paper
Large spoon *or* soup spoon
2 mixing bowls
Electric mixer *or* potato masher *or* ricer
Oven-proof serving platter *or* dish

FOODS YOU WILL NEED:
Large oval-shaped baking potatoes—
   ½ for each serving
For each potato:
   1½ tablespoons butter *or* margarine
   2 tablespoons cream *or* milk *or*
     sour cream
   ⅛ teaspoon salt
   Dash of pepper
   1 teaspoon chopped chives *or*
     dill (optional)
   2 tablespoons grated Cheddar cheese
   Dash of paprika (optional)

Ingredients:

(Plan on ½ potato for each serving)

Baking potatoes
Butter

How To:

1. Turn oven on to 350°.

2. Wash potato skins well, then dry them on a towel. Poke fork a little way into side of each whole potato to make holes for steam to escape. Rub a little butter over outside of each potato.

3. Place potatoes on oven rack. Set timer for 45 minutes. While potatoes bake, prepare other ingredients.

FOR EACH
WHOLE POTATO:
1 tablespoon butter *or*
  margarine
2 tablespoons cream *or* milk
  or sour cream
⅛ teaspoon salt
Dash of pepper
1 teaspoon finely chopped
  fresh (or ½ teaspoon
  dried) chives *or* dill
  (optional)

2 tablespoons grated
  Cheddar cheese

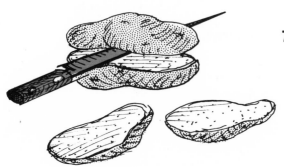

4. For each *whole* potato, add to small saucepan the specified amount of butter *or* margarine, milk *or* cream *or* sour cream, salt, and pepper. Add chives *and/or* dill as well if you like them. Set pan over low heat and warm until butter melts. Then remove from heat and set aside.

5. On wax paper, grate (or finely slice) about 2 tablespoons cheese for each whole potato. Set cheese aside.

6. After 45 minutes, hold potatoes with potholder and remove them from oven. Test doneness by piercing potatoes with knife. Blade should slide through easily. If potatoes are still too hard, return them to oven to bake about 15 minutes longer. When done, turn off oven. Set potatoes aside to cool.

7. When cool enough to handle, slice each potato in half lengthwise.

8. With spoon, scoop potato pulp out of skins into mixing bowl. Leave skins about ⅛" thick. Take care not to tear skins; they should be whole so they can later be stuffed.

9. To mash pulp, either beat it in bowl with electric mixer, *or* masher, *or* spoon it into opened ricer. To use ricer, pull down handle, forcing pulp out into the second mixing bowl.

10. Add the warmed butter-and-milk mixture to mashed-potato pulp. With spoon, stir mixture together well. Preheat broiler.

11. Spoon potato mixture into each half-skin, mounding the potato a little on top. Set stuffed boats on oven-proof serving platter.

12. Sprinkle about 1 tablespoon of your grated or sliced cheese over top of each boat. Also top with a dash of paprika, if you like.

Paprika (optional)

13. Set platter under broiler for about 4 to 5 minutes, or until cheese melts and begins to turn golden brown. Serve hot.

RICE WREATH

This unusual rice dish looks very festive on a Christmas party table. It is molded in the shape of a wreath and trimmed with sweet red pepper stars. Fill the wreath's center with cooked peas and complete the decorations with an outer ring of peas or whole cherry tomatoes. Serve with a meat dish such as Shish Kebab (see index). NOTE: This is a good recipe for several cooks to work on together, each one preparing a different ingredient. There are two steps where you may need the help of an adult.

EQUIPMENT:
Large and small saucepans, with lids
Measuring cups and spoons
Timer
9″ ring mold (if you do not want a
    wreath shape, use any 6-cup
    mold)
Wax paper
Paring knife
Wooden spoon *or* large spoon
Fork
Rubber scraper
Roasting pan—large enough to hold
    ring mold inside it
2 potholders
Table knife
Flat serving platter—at least 2 or more
inches larger around than ring
    mold (if dish is to be kept warm in
    oven, platter should be oven-proof)
Colander (only needed if cooking peas)

FOODS YOU WILL NEED:
4½ cups water
2 cups uncooked whole-grain white rice
1 teaspoon salt
½ cup (1 stick) plus 2 tablespoons
    butter *or* margarine
½ cup chopped fresh parsley *or*
    3 tablespoons dried parsley
1 6- or 7-ounce jar sweet roasted
    peppers *or* 2 whole sweet red
    peppers *or* tomatoes
2 or 3 cups fresh (shelled) *or* frozen peas

Ingredients:

(To make about 10 to 12 servings. NOTE: To make less, cut recipe in half and use smaller mold.)

4 cups water
2 cups uncooked whole-grain
    white rice
½ teaspoon salt
1 tablespoon butter

How To:

1. Make rice according to your favorite recipe, or follow our directions: Combine water, rice, salt, and butter in large saucepan. Cover with lid and place over high heat. Bring to boil.

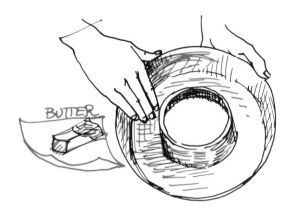

Butter

¼ cup (½ stick) butter *or* margarine

½ cup chopped fresh parsley *or* 3 tablespoons dried parsley

Sweet roasted peppers (one 6- or 7-ounce jar, sold in grocery stores) *or* fresh sweet red peppers *or* fresh tomato skins with pulp removed

PEPPERS

2. As soon as water boils, immediately turn heat down to very low. Set timer for 25 minutes and simmer rice, covered. Do not lift lid. This keeps steam inside pot so it can be absorbed by rice. While rice is cooking, prepare mold and other ingredients.

3. Turn oven on to 375°. Spread butter generously all over the inside of ring mold and set it aside.

4. Measure butter *or* margarine into small saucepan. Set it over very low heat until butter is melted. Remove from heat and set it aside.

5. Measure parsley onto wax paper and set it aside.

6. With paring knife, cut peppers into about 12 strips, each 3″ to 4″ long and ⅛″ to ¼″ wide. Set them aside on wax paper.

7. Check timing of rice. After 25 minutes, all water should be absorbed. At that point, uncover rice and taste it. If grains feel *just* cooked through when you bite them, and they look separate (not wet and mushy) in the pan, rice is done. Remove rice from heat. However, if all water is gone and grains of rice are still too hard to bite through, add 2 to 4 tablespoons water, cover, and simmer a few more minutes over low heat. If rice looks too wet, remove lid and simmer *uncovered* for 3 to 5 minutes. Rice will later be baked in mold, so it should not be overcooked now.

8. Sprinkle parsley over cooked rice and stir it in with spoon or fork.

9. Spoon rice into buttered mold. Pack rice down firmly with back of spoon.

10. Pour melted butter *or* margarine evenly over rice in mold. Use rubber scraper to remove all butter from pan.

11. In roasting pan, add hot tap water to a depth of about 1″. Then gently set filled mold into pan with rice facing up. Water should reach about 1″ up outside of mold. If there is not enough water, add more—a cupful at a time—being careful not to get water in the rice.

12. Cut a piece of wax paper slightly wider than ring mold—10″ to 12″. Set it aside for next step.

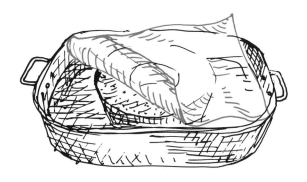

2 or 3 cups fresh *or* frozen peas

½ cup water

Pinch of salt
2 teaspoons butter

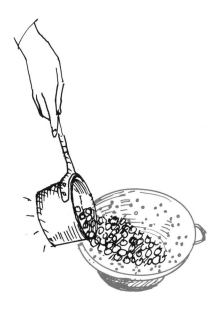

13. *You may need to ask an adult to help you with this step.* Very carefully, because it is heavy, set pan containing water and mold into center of pre-heated oven. Place piece of wax paper over top of mold. Set timer for 20 minutes.

14. While rice is baking, cook peas (or any other vegetable you might prefer) to fill center of wreath.

15. To cook peas, add water to saucepan in which butter was melted for rice. Cover and bring to boil over high heat. Add peas. Return water to boil, then immediately lower heat to simmer and cover. Set timer to 3 or 4 minutes for frozen peas, 6 or 7 minutes—or until tender—for fresh peas. Turn off heat.

16. *Carefully*, with potholder, carry pan to sink and drain peas through colander. (For good nutrition, you can save this water to use in a soup.) Place pan lid over peas in colander to keep them warm.

17. *You may need to ask an adult to help you with this step.* After rice has baked 20 minutes, turn off oven. Remove wax paper from top of mold. Then, using potholders, carefully lift mold out of water and remove it from oven. Or, if it is easier, remove roasting pan from oven first, then remove mold from pan. (Be sure to set hot pans on heat-proof surface.) Run blade of table knife carefully around edge of rice to loosen it from mold.

18. Set serving platter upside down over top of mold. With potholders against mold, pick up both platter and mold *at the same time* and turn them upside down. Set platter down on table and gently lift mold straight up and off rice. (If rice does not slide out easily, tap bottom of mold lightly with back of knife.)

19. Trim rice by draping pepper strips over wreath or making stars by crossing 3 strips over each other at evenly spaced intervals on wreath top.

20. Fill center of wreath with hot peas topped with a pinch of salt and 2 teaspoons butter. If peas are cold, reheat them quickly in small saucepan with a few tablespoons of water. Drain, then add peas to wreath.

21. Serve immediately, while rice is hot. (To keep dish warm, cover with aluminum foil or, if platter is oven-proof, place in 175° to 200° oven for a few minutes.)

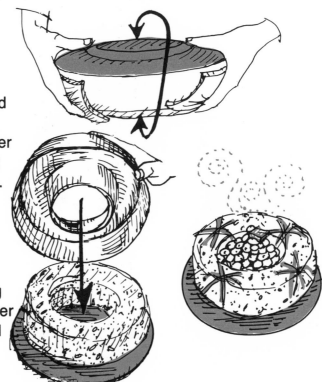

GREEN NOODLES WITH CHEESE SAUCE

This Italian dish is easy to prepare and may be served as a main course for lunch, with a salad or whole cherry tomatoes. It is also good as a side dish for dinner with Fried Chicken (see index) and a salad or sliced tomatoes. NOTE: This recipe can also be made with plain white noodles.

EQUIPMENT:
Frying pan
Long-handled fork *or* tongs
Large pot with lid
Mixing bowl
Measuring cups and spoons
Eggbeater *or* wire whisk
Paper towels *or* brown paper bag
Grater (optional)
Wax paper
Timer
2 potholders
Colander
Wooden spoon
Oven-proof serving platter
Rubber scraper

FOODS YOU WILL NEED:
8 strips bacon
4 quarts water
1 egg
½ cup light cream *or* milk
1½ teaspoons salt
½ teaspoon pepper
¾ cup grated Parmesan cheese *or*
  ¼-pound piece of solid cheese
4 tablespoons butter
1 tablespoon cooking oil
12-ounce *or* 1-pound package spinach
  egg noodles *or* plain *linguine or*
  fettucine noodles

Ingredients:

(To make 8 servings)

8 strips bacon

4 quarts (16 cups) water

How To:

1. Place bacon in frying pan and set on stove over *low* heat. Watch bacon carefully while preparing rest of recipe. Occasionally, turn strips very carefully and slowly with long-handled fork *or* tongs.

2. Measure water into large pot and cover. Set over high heat and bring to a boil. While waiting for water to boil, prepare sauce as follows.

1 egg
½ cup light cream *or* milk
1 teaspoon salt
½ teaspoon pepper, pref-
erably freshly ground

¾ cup grated Parmesan
cheese *or* about ¼-pound
piece of solid cheese
4 tablespoons butter

½ teaspoon salt
1 tablespoon cooking oil
12-ounce *or* 1-pound package
spinach egg noodles
(*or* substitute plain *linguine*
or fettucine noodles)

ADD NOODLES BY
STANDING THEM UP
IN POT

3. Break egg into mixing bowl. Add cream *or* milk, salt, and pepper and beat thoroughly with eggbeater *or* whisk. NOTE: Don't forget to check on bacon and remove it from heat when cooked. When bacon is crisp, remove pan from heat. Transfer bacon to paper towels *or* brown paper bag to drain.

4. If your cheese is in a solid piece, grate ¾ cup of it onto wax paper *or* into measuring cup. Cut 4 tablespoons butter into small chunks and set them on top of cheese. Put aside.

5. Crumble cooked and drained bacon into small pieces on wax paper and set it aside.

6. When water is boiling rapidly, remove lid and add salt and oil. Then, *carefully*, so you don't get splashed, add noodles to pot. Set timer and boil noodles, uncovered, about 6 to 7 minutes. Once or twice during cooking, stir noodles with fork so they do not stick together. (Spinach noodles will cook faster than *linguine* or *fettucine*.)

(57)

7. To test for doneness, use long-handled fork to fish a noodle out of the water. Use potholder to hold pot steady with one hand while you do this. Bite into noodle. It should feel slightly firm (*al dente*, which means "to the tooth" in Italian). It is better for the noodles to be a tiny bit undercooked than soggy. When done, turn off heat under pot.

8. While noodles are cooking, you can warm your serving platter or plates. Set in a 175° oven for 3 to 4 minutes or rinse under very hot water, then dry and set aside.

9. When noodles are cooked, set colander in sink. *You may need to ask an adult to help you with this step.* Hold pot handles with potholders and *carefully and slowly* carry pot to sink. Hold your face to one side to avoid the steam. Pour contents of pot into colander to drain.

10. When water has drained from noodles, pour them back into empty pot. Do *not* return pot to stove.

11. Immediately, assemble dish while noodles are still very hot. To do this, pour butter-cheese mixture over noodles and toss with wooden spoon until butter starts to melt. Then add egg-cream mixture and mix well. Sauce should be very creamy.

12. Pour noodles and sauce out onto warmed serving platter or plates. Remove sauce from sides of pan with rubber scraper. Sprinkle crumbled bacon over top. Serve immediately. NOTE: Do not reheat noodles or egg will cook and sauce will become dry.

Main-Dish Meats

MEATBALLS IN PASTRY POCKETS

This dish begins very simply and ends as a very special treat. The hamburger mixture can be turned into meatloaf or plain meatballs, or baked in squares of rich dough. These delicious meat pastries are very much like the Russian specialty known as *piroshki*. They are quite easy to make, and the praise you receive will make you feel like an accomplished cook. Serve the pastries as bite-sized hot appetizers at a party, or as a main dish with a vegetable such as Peas in Tomato Shells (see index) and a salad. NOTE: If you are going to do the pastry, it should be made first, then chilled in the refrigerator while the meat is being prepared.

Pastries may be reheated the next day (if you are lucky enough to have any left). Place them in a baking pan in a preheated 350° oven for about 5 to 8 minutes, or until they are hot through. To freeze baked pastries, cool them completely, then wrap in airtight aluminum foil *or* a plastic bag, *or* both.

EQUIPMENT:
Large fork and spoon
Electric mixer (optional)
2 large mixing bowls
Measuring cup and spoons
Sifter
Wax paper
Garlic press
Large oven-proof serving platter
   (about 14" long)
Soup bowl
Knife
Rolling pin
Ruler
Spatula *or* pancake turner
Jelly roll pan *or* cookie sheet with
   edge all around *or* baking pan
Pastry brush
Timer
Potholders

FOODS YOU WILL NEED:
8 ounces cream cheese
8 ounces (2 sticks) butter (*not*
   margarine)
2 cups all-purpose flour
½ cup bread crumbs *or* 1 slice white
   or whole wheat bread
¼ cup milk
2 eggs
1 pound ordinary hamburger (preferably
   an inexpensive grind containing
   some fat to add needed moisture
   to the meatballs)
1 small clove garlic
2 tablespoons finely chopped onion
¼ cup wheat germ
½ teaspoon dried oregano *or* thyme *or*
   2 teaspoons dried *or* 2 tablespoons
   fresh dill
½ teaspoon salt
2 pinches of pepper

CREAM CHEESE PASTRY

Because this recipe contains so much butter and cream cheese, it is very easy to handle and will make a moist pastry that goes well with the meat filling. (Margarine cannot be substituted for butter here; it is too soft.) If you prefer, however, you can make any regular 2-crust pie dough, though it will tend to be drier and harder to handle for this purpose.

Ingredients:

(To make about 36 pastry pockets or 2 crusts for 8" or 9" pie)

8 ounces cream cheese, *at room temperature*

8 ounces (2 sticks) butter, (*not* margarine), *at room temperature*

2 cups all-purpose flour

How To:

1. Wash your hands. With a fork, cut cream cheese and butter into small pieces in the mixing bowl. Blend ingredients together with fork *or* electric mixer.

2. Sift measured flour directly over mixture in bowl. Blend with fork or fingers until you form a smooth dough, but do *not* overwork it. Add a tiny bit more flour if dough feels too sticky to handle.

3. Wrap ball of dough in wax paper and chill in refrigerator until meat mixture is prepared. You will use pastry in step 6 of meatball recipe.

MEAT FILLING

Ingredients:

How To:

(To make about 36 meat-balls, 1" in diameter. Serve 4 to 6 pastry-wrapped meatballs to each person for a main course.)

½ cup bread crumbs *or* 1 slice white *or* whole wheat bread
¼ cup milk

1 egg

1. Turn oven on to 375°. Wash your hands.

2. Soak bread or bread crumbs in milk in mixing bowl. When soft, stir with a fork.

3. Break egg into a measuring cup, then add it to bread-milk mixture and stir.

1 pound hamburger
1 small clove garlic
2 tablespoons finely chopped onion
¼ cup wheat germ
½ teaspoon dried oregano *or* thyme *or* 2 teaspoons dried dill
½ teaspoon salt
2 pinches of pepper, preferably freshly ground

4. In the same bowl, add hamburger, crumbled up with your fingers so it is in small pieces. Put garlic through press (see Basic Skills) and add it to hamburger. Add chopped onion (see Basic Skills), wheat germ, oregano *or* thyme *or* dill, salt, and pepper. Mix everything together with fork or with your hands until well blended.

5. Cut a piece of wax paper about 12″ to 14″ long and set it nearby. Use all the meat mixture to make about 36 meatballs, roughly 1″ in diameter (walnut-sized). Place meatballs side by side on the wax paper. Set wax paper on large serving platter and place in the refrigerator. Chill meat while pastry is being rolled out.

6. Now you are ready to use the prepared pastry. Cut a 14″ length of wax paper and flour it lightly. Remove *half* the pastry dough from the refrigerator, leaving the rest there to chill until needed. Sprinkle a little flour on top of the dough, then cover it with a second 14″-long piece of wax paper.

7. Roll out dough between the 2 papers until it is about ⅛″ thick. Be sure dough is not too thick.

8. Break one egg into soup bowl and beat it with fork. Place nearby.

9. Remove top paper from rolled dough. Use knife to cut dough into 3″ squares. Dip knife in flour if it sticks.

10. Remove half the meat from refrigerator, leaving the rest there to chill until needed.

11. Dip spatula into flour, then lift 1 dough square at a time onto *ungreased* baking pan.

12. Place 1 meatball in the center of each dough square. To form dough envelope or pocket, pull up and pinch together 2 opposite corners as shown. Then pinch together the remaining corners. Finally, pinch side edges closed. Add a drop of beaten egg with your finger if needed to make dough stick together.

13. Arrange pockets about 1″ apart on pan. Dip pastry brush

in egg, then brush tops of dough pockets.

14. Repeat steps 6 to 13, using up rest of chilled pastry dough and meat mixture, as well as beaten egg. Wash platter and set it aside.

15. Set timer for 30 minutes, bake pastry at 375°. Check at the end of this time; pastry should be light golden brown. If it is not, reset timer to bake 10 minutes longer. When pastry is done, turn off oven. Use potholders and be careful to hold baking pan level when removing it from the oven because there may be some hot fat in the bottom. Set serving platter in oven for 3 to 4 minutes to warm. Remove with potholders.

16. Use spatula *or* pancake turner to lift pockets onto warmed platter. Serve hot.

VARIATIONS:

Plain Meatballs: Do not make pastry. Prepare meatballs as described above, or make them even larger, about 1½" to 2" in diameter. Heat 2 tablespoons butter or oil in frying pan, then add meatballs. You may have to do this in 2 batches, so pan will not be overcrowded. Cook over medium heat, turning with spatula *or* wooden spoon. Cook from 7 to 15 minutes, or until meat has lost its pink color. Time will depend on size of meatballs. Keep first batch warm on oven-proof platter in 200° oven while cooking the rest. Serve hot with Scandinavian Yule Red Cabbage and Rice Wreath (see index).

Meatloaf: Prepare meat mixture through step 4. Place meat in 9" × 5" × 2¾" (or smaller) loaf pan, patting it in so it is at least 2½" to 2¾" thick. If meat is too thin when spread over bottom of entire pan, push it up toward one end until thick enough. Cover meat with 2 or 3 tablespoons of any tomato sauce or catsup and 2 slices of bacon. Bake in 350° oven for 45 to 50 minutes, or until meat loses its red color. Spoon off fat. Use spatula to cut into 5 slices, each about ¾" thick. Serve on warm platter with Stuffed Potato Boats and Peas in Tomato Shells (see index).

FRIED CHICKEN

This is an easy recipe that produces delicious results: fried chicken in both a plain and a fancy version—Chicken Continental. There are several different activities involved in the preparation, so this is a good project for several cooks to work on together.

EQUIPMENT:
Medium-sized mixing bowl
Measuring cups and spoons
Eggbeater *or* whisk
Lunch-bag-size paper *or* plastic bag
Wax paper
Large (12″) frying pan (with lid, if making Chicken Continental)
Long-handled fork *or* tongs
Spoon
Spatula (optional)
Oven-proof serving platter
Paper towels
Potholders
Kitchen knife
Small jar *or* soup bowl (optional)

FOODS YOU WILL NEED:
2 eggs
½ teaspoon salt
½ teaspoon pepper
1 teaspoon Worcestershire *or* soy sauce
⅔ cup all-purpose whole wheat *or* white flour
¼ cup wheat germ
3 tablespoons grated Parmesan cheese
2 whole chicken breasts, cut in half (4 pieces) *or* 1 whole chicken, cut in serving pieces
⅔ cup vegetable oil *or* margarine
bread (optional)

For Chicken Continental only:
6 thin slices boiled ham
½ pound thinly sliced mozzarella *or* Swiss cheese
Oregano *or* thyme, fresh *or* dried
¾ cup chicken broth *or* heavy *or* light cream *or* milk

Ingredients:

(To make 4 to 6 servings)

2 eggs
½ teaspoon salt
½ teaspoon pepper
1 teaspoon Worcestershire *or* soy sauce
⅔ cup all-purpose whole wheat *or* white flour
¼ cup wheat germ
3 tablespoons grated Parmesan cheese

How To:

1. Break eggs into mixing bowl. Add salt, pepper, and sauce. Beat well.

2. Measure flour, wheat germ, and grated cheese into paper *or* plastic bag. Shake bag to mix.

2 whole chicken breasts,
cut in half *or* 1 whole
chicken, cut in serving
pieces

⅔ cup vegetable oil *or*
margarine
Small piece of bread (optional)

3. Cut a piece of wax paper and set it on counter. Dip each piece of chicken into the egg mixture, then drop it gently into the bag of flour mixture. Close top of bag, then shake it gently until chicken is coated. Set chicken on wax paper and repeat with other pieces.

4. Add oil *or* margarine to frying pan. Set pan on stove over medium heat. Heat oil until a drop of flour batter or a piece of bread bubbles up and browns quickly when dropped in it. When oil is ready, use tongs *or* long-handled fork to add chicken. *Do not drop* chicken in or grease will splatter.

5. Cook chicken 4 to 5 minutes, or until bottom is browned, then turn.

6. When browned, lower heat and cook chicken slowly, uncovered, about 30 minutes, or until the thickest pieces of chicken feel soft all the way through when stuck with the fork.

7. Remove cooked chicken from pan and place it on a platter lined with paper towels. When grease is drained, remove papers and serve chicken immediately.

CHICKEN CONTINENTAL

Ingredients:

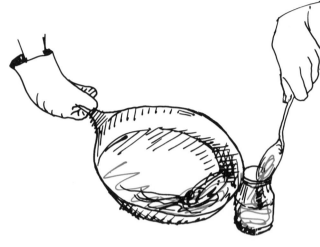

6 thin slices boiled ham
½ pound thinly sliced
   mozzarella *or* Swiss
   cheese
Oregano *or* thyme, fresh
   or dried

¾ cup chicken broth *or*
   heavy *or* light cream *or*
   milk

How To:

1. Make Fried Chicken, steps 1 to 6. When chicken is cooked, use tongs *or* fork to transfer it to a platter. Hold pan with potholder and spoon oil *or* margarine out of frying pan and into a small bowl *or* jar. Return chicken to frying pan. (NOTE: Oil can be strained and used again.)

2. Use knife to slice ham and cheese. Place 1 slice, or part of a slice, of ham over each piece of chicken. Cover ham with a slice of cheese. Sprinkle oregano *or* thyme lightly over cheese.

3. Pour liquid over chicken. Cover pan with lid and set over low heat to simmer slowly until cheese melts (about 5 minutes). Spoon pan gravy over chicken. Serve chicken from pan, covering each piece with pan gravy.

SHISH KEBAB

Everyone loves this dish, whose name combines the Turkish words *şiş* (skewer) and *kebap* (roast meat). A Middle Eastern specialty, Shish Kebab is colorful to look at, fun to prepare (let your guests help), and easy to cook on an outdoor grill, in the fireplace, or in the oven broiler.

Make your kebabs with beef or lamb, and any combination of vegetables you like. The marinade and the fire help to create a unique flavor that will go well with a Rice Wreath (see index), a green salad, and French or Syrian bread. To be really authentic, serve Shish Kebab with a side dish of plain yogurt.

EQUIPMENT:
Roasting pan *or* large bowl
Wax paper
Paring knife
4 skewers—each at least 12″ long, with a turning ring or hook on one end. The best skewers are made of oblong rods with angles that will grip the food and keep it from sliding; some rods are also twisted in order to hold food well
Wax paper *or* jelly roll pan
Pastry brush
Outdoor charcoal grill *or* hibachi *or* oven broiler
Tongs *or* long-handled fork

Potholders
Oven-proof serving platter

FOODS YOU WILL NEED:
1 pound cubed lean lamb *or* cubed boneless beef (top round *or* sirloin, for example)
Juice of 1½ lemons
2 tablespoons salad oil
½ to 1 teaspoon dried oregano
1 teaspoon dried mint leaves (optional, for lamb only)
Pinch of salt
Pinch of pepper
2 whole medium-sized green peppers
16 whole cherry *or* 8 small tomatoes

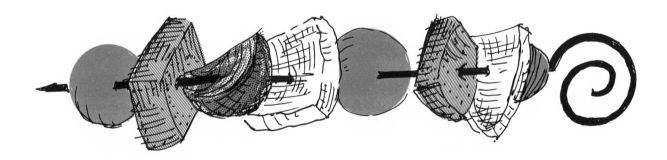

Ingredients:

(To make 4 servings)

1 pound cubed lamb *or* beef;
  cubes cut about 1″ × 1½″
Juice of 1½ lemons (pits
  removed)
2 tablespoons salad oil
½ to 1 teaspoon dried
  oregano
1 teaspoon dried mint—for
  lamb only (optional)
Pinch of salt
Pinch of pepper, preferably
  freshly ground

2 green peppers
16 cherry *or* 8 small
  tomatoes

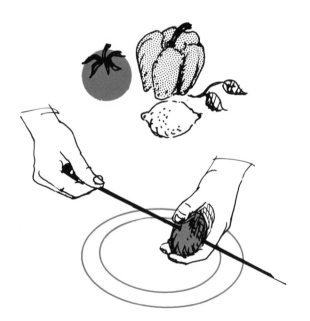

How To:

1. The night (or at least 1 hour) before you plan to cook the kebabs, place the meat in a marinade. Make this by combining the meat with lemon juice, oil, and spices in roasting pan *or* bowl. Turn meat around to coat it well, cover it with wax paper, and refrigerate until ready to thread on skewers.

2. Wash peppers and tomatoes. Cut peppers in half, remove core, seeds, and white ribs. Cut the peppers into approximately 1½″ squares. Pick leaves and stems off tomatoes. Leave cherry tomatoes whole; cut small regular tomatoes in half.

3. Thread skewer by pushing the pointed end through the center of each piece in turn. Alternate items, adding meat first, then pepper, then tomato, then meat again. Try to push through the center of the tomato, so it will not fall off when cooked. Repeat,

threading to within about 1″ of end. Thread all skewers and set them on wax paper *or* jelly roll pan.

A 12″ skewer holds about 5 cubes of meat, 4 tomatoes, and 4 pepper squares—and makes 1 serving.

4. Use pastry brush to coat entire length of each skewer with marinade left in bowl that held meat.

5. Set skewers about 3″ from heat source on prepared (hot) grill, hibachi, *or* broiler rack (with a pan underneath). Broil about 5 minutes. Turn skewers, holding hooked ends with potholder. Brush skewers again with marinade.

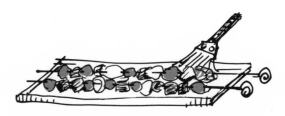

6. Broil 7 to 10 minutes more, or more or less, depending on how rare you like your meat and how thick the cubes are. Cut into a piece of meat after the first 10 minutes, to test doneness.

7. Brush marinade over skewers from time to time, while cooking. Remember that skewered foods cook quickly, and beef and lamb are both most tender when still pink inside. Set oven-proof platter in oven to warm for a few minutes. Then use potholders to remove platter from oven.

8. When done, hold skewers with potholder, remove them from grill, and set them on warmed platter. Use tongs *or* fork to slide meat and vegetables off skewer. Serve hot.

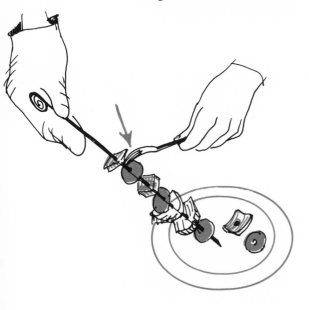

Treats and Sweets

MARZIPAN

Marzipan candy is a Christmas and New Year specialty in many European countries. Brightly colored fruit and vegetable shapes are popular, but one of the most unusual shapes is found in Austria, where the marzipan pig is a favorite treat. The pig is the symbol of good luck and a fat future because he digs for his food in a forward direction with such success. To bring extra good fortune, you can place a gold-foil coin *or* a paper four-leaf clover in his mouth, or tie a red ribbon around his belly and hang the pig on your Christmas tree. Marzipan is easy to make, and in any shape it will surely bring you a delicious and lucky New Year.

Marzipan candy is made from almond paste, which is a mixture of ground almonds, egg whites, and sugar. Some stores sell canned almond paste, but it can be quite expensive and is often hard to find. It is very easy to make your own by following the recipe below. This is a good group project, for several cooks can share in the mixing and modeling of the marzipan candies.

EQUIPMENT:
Measuring cups and spoons
Saucepan with lid
Strainer
Potholder
Jelly roll pan *or* cookie sheet with
    edges *or* 10″ × 14″ sheet of aluminum
    foil with edges turned up
Timer
Blender *or* food *or* nut mill with fine nut
    disk *or* meat grinder with finest blade
Rubber scraper
Large and medium-sized mixing bowls
Small bowls *or* cups—one for each
    color you plan to tint the marzipan
Wax paper
Plastic wrap *or* plastic bag

Toothpicks
New small paint brush
Scissors
Green construction paper (optional)
Small paring knife
Gold *or* silver foil (optional)

FOODS YOU WILL NEED:
1 8-ounce can (1 cup) pure almond
    paste *or* 1 cup whole almonds
    (blanched *or* with skins on)
water
2 egg whites
3½ to 4 cups confectioners' sugar
2 teaspoons almond extract
Vegetable food coloring
Powdered cocoa (optional)

ALMONDS
SKINS ON

BLANCHED

Ingredients:

(To make about 2 cups Marzipan, which makes about 40 candies 1" in diameter)

1 8-ounce can (1 cup) pure almond paste (see note in step 1) *or* 1 cup whole blanched (white) almonds. (If your almonds are blanched, go to step 6.) If your almonds have their brown skins on, follow steps 2 through 5 to remove (blanch) them.

3 cups water

How To:

1. Turn on oven to 200°. NOTE: If using canned almond paste, go directly to * in NOTE at end of recipe.

2. To blanch almonds, place about 3 cups water in a saucepan. Cover pan and set it on stove. Bring water to a boil.

3. Remove cover from pan. Gently add nuts to water without splashing. Boil nuts, uncovered, about 2 minutes. While nuts are boiling, set strainer in medium-sized bowl in sink.

4. Turn off heat under pan. Hold pan handle with potholder and *carefully and slowly* carry pan to sink. Pour contents of pan through strainer.

5. Return strained nuts to pan and cover them with cold water. When nuts are cooled off, pinch them between your fingers. The skins will slip off easily as the nuts pop out. Brothers and sisters love to help out with this step!

6. Spread out skinless (blanched) nuts on jelly roll pan *or* cookie sheet *or* foil and set them in the oven at 200°. Set timer for 5 minutes. This will dry out the nuts so they can be ground easily. Even if you are using nuts that were blanched when you bought them, grinding will be easier if they are dried out.

7. Remove nuts from the oven and let them cool. Then put them through a meat grinder *or* food *or* nut mill *or* whirl them in a blender (following step 8).

To use a meat grinder, set a bowl *or* piece of wax paper under grinding disk. Put a few nuts at a time into top hole, push them down with dry crust of bread (*not* your fingers), and turn handle.

To use food *or* nut mill, hold it over wax paper. Lift presser bar and put some nuts on cutting disk. Replace bar and press it down onto nuts while turning handle.

8. If using a blender, add only ½ cup nuts at a time. Blend about 4 seconds, or until nuts seem packed against container sides. Then *remove container from motor base*. With rubber scraper, stir up nuts stuck to container bottom. *Never reach inside container while it sits on motor; blades are dangerous.* Nuts should be quite finely ground, with no big chunks left. After stirring, cover container and put blender back on again for a few seconds. Repeat about 3 times in all, or until nuts are evenly and finely ground. Empty nuts into large mixing bowl and repeat procedure to grind second ½ cup of nuts.

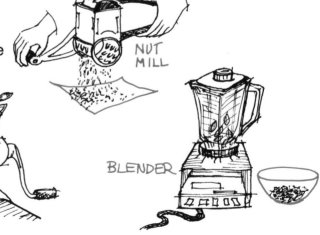

NUT MILL

MEAT GRINDER

BLENDER

2 egg whites

3½ to 4 cups *unsifted*
   confectioners' sugar
2 teaspoons almond extract

Confectioners' sugar

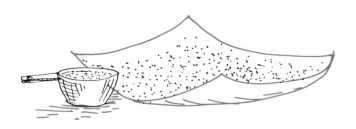

9. Separate eggs (see Basic Skills). Put yolks in a cup *or* small bowl and set them aside for some other use.

10. Pour egg whites into large bowl with ground nuts. Add 3½ cups sugar and almond extract.

11. Stop and wash your hands.

12. Coat your hands with confectioners' sugar, then use your hands to mix up all ingredients until they form a well-blended ball of dough. Add ¼ to ½ cup more sugar if mixture feels too sticky. The amount of sugar needed depends upon the size of the eggs used. Add sugar to bowl and squeeze; knead and fold over dough in bowl until it feels like rolled cookie dough. It should be easy to mold or roll between your fingers, but not so dry that it crumbles.

13. Cut a piece of wax paper about 14″ long. Set it on work surface and sprinkle it with confectioners' sugar.

14. Turn ball of marzipan dough out onto the paper. Knead dough a few times by folding it and pushing it away from you with the heel of your hand.

15. Cover ball of dough with plastic wrap *or* wax paper, *or* place it in a plastic bag. Take out only when you are ready to use; dough will dry out when exposed to the air.

Marzipan at this stage can also be divided into small portions, wrapped in airtight plastic bags, and frozen. Bring dough to room temperature before modeling shapes.

16. Shape fruits as shown, modeling them as you would clay. To stick 2 pieces together, add a drop of water at the point where they touch.

17. To prepare colors for painting on dough, place a few drops of vegetable food coloring in cups. Dilute colors with a few drops of water if they look too dark.

18. Set shaped candies on clean piece of wax paper. Use small new brush to paint on colors. When first color is dry, add details with toothpick *or* brush dipped in another color.

To color marzipan all the way through, add a few drops of color directly to a lump of dough. Knead and squeeze dough until color is evenly distributed throughout, then shape.

(74)

19. Make stem for apple *or* strawberry with half toothpick painted with green food coloring. Make leaves of cut green paper and poke stem toothpicks through them.

20. Shape pig as shown. Cut open mouth with knife. Cut out gold- *or* silver-foil coin and stick it into pig's mouth.

Powdered cocoa (optional)

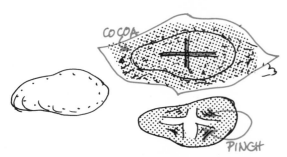

21. To make a potato, form an oval ball of dough. Roll ball in cocoa. Cut cross in top with scissors *or* knife. Pinch sides of cross to open top.

22. Let candies dry in air several hours or overnight. Then store them in an airtight container *or* wrap them in plastic wrap.

NOTE: The method described above makes a very good quick marzipan. However, if you have the time, the more traditional method is to make an almond *paste* first by combining all the ground almonds with 1 egg white and 1½ to 2 cups confectioners' sugar. This is blended into a fairly dry dough, wrapped in wax paper, and left overnight (or for several hours) in the refrigerator for the flavor to "ripen." The next day, blend in 1 egg white, 2 teaspoons almond extract, and 2 to 2½ cups confectioners' sugar. Shape candies.

⟶ *Canned almond paste can be used in place of your homemade paste. To turn it into marzipan candy, crumble it in a bowl. Then add 1 egg white, 2 teaspoons almond extract, and about 2 to 2½ cups confectioners' sugar. Blend well. Color and shape candies as in steps 16 to 22.

 **FRENCH CHOCOLATE TRUFFLES**

There are many types of truffles, but the best-tasting come from France. The truffle, which grows under the ground, is an edible member of the fungus family. These candies are called after the truffle because they are round in shape, dark in color, velvety in texture, and heavenly in taste.

EQUIPMENT:
Jelly roll pan *or* roasting pan *or* cookie sheet with edges
Timer
Measuring cups and spoons
Double boiler
Small saucepan
Large mixing bowl
Potholders
Wooden spoon
2 heat-proof pads *or* trivets
Blender *or* nut grinder
Teacup
Rubber scraper

Soup bowls—1 for each type of truffle coating
Wax paper
Airtight container

FOODS YOU WILL NEED:
1 cup pecans *or* walnuts *or* hazelnuts (without shells)
2 cups (12 ounces) semisweet chocolate bits
¼ cup light *or* heavy cream
1¼ cups confectioners' sugar
1 egg white
Optional truffle coating—(see ingredients list in recipe)

Ingredients:

(*To make about 60 truffles, 1" in diameter*)

1 cup pecans *or* walnuts *or* hazelnuts (without shells)

How To:

1. Wash your hands, as you will be using them to mold truffles. Turn oven on to 200°.

2. Spread nuts out in jelly roll *or* other pan and place them in the oven. Set timer for 5 minutes. This will dry out nuts so they can be ground easily.

2 cups (12 ounces) semisweet
chocolate bits

¼ cup light *or* heavy cream

1¼ cups confectioners'
sugar

MIX WITH WOODEN
SPOON OR HANDS

3. While nuts are drying, measure chocolate into the top section of a double boiler. Put about 1½″ to 2″ of water in the bottom of the pot, set it on the stove, and bring it to a boil. Then place section containing chocolate over the boiling water. Turn heat down slightly and let water simmer under chocolate until it is melted.

4. Measure cream into small saucepan and set it on stove over low heat to warm. When warm, turn off stove under pan.

5. Measure sugar into large mixing bowl.

6. When nuts are done, remove them from oven and let cool. When chocolate is melted, turn off stove under it. Remove top section of double boiler from heat.

7. Put cool nuts through a nut grinder *or* in the blender. If using a blender, add only ½ cup nuts at a time. Whirl until finely ground, following directions for Marzipan (see index), steps 7 and 8. Add ground nuts to sugar in bowl.

1 egg white

CREAM + CHOCOLATE

Coating—1 or more of the
following:
  ½ cup granulated sugar
  ½ cup sweetened cocoa
  (regular *or* instant type)
  ½ cup dried coconut
  ½ cup finely chopped
  nuts
  ½ cup chocolate shot
  or "sprinkles"

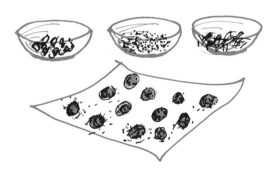

8. Separate the egg (see Basic
Skills) and add the white to
the nut-sugar mixture in bowl.
Place yolk in teacup and
save for another use. Work
egg white into sugar and
nuts until it becomes
quite stiff.

9. Pour warm cream into melted
chocolate and blend with
wooden spoon until smooth.
Use rubber scraper to empty
chocolate mixture into bowl
containing nuts, sugar, and
egg white. Use your hands to
work the ingredients until
well blended.

10. Set out 1 *or* more soup bowls
containing truffle coatings:
sugar, cocoa, coconut,
nuts, *or* chocolate shot. Cut
a sheet of wax paper approximately 14″ long and set it
beside the bowls.

11. Pick up small lumps of warm
chocolate mixture and roll
them into 1″ balls.

12. Roll each chocolate ball in
one of the coatings, then set
ball on wax paper to dry until
hard. This will take 3 to 4
hours. Turn truffles once or
twice while drying. Store
truffles in airtight container.

ORANGE-NUT SUGARPLUMS

This Christmas, you can have real sugarplums instead of just visions dancing in your head. Although these hard-nut candies don't contain any plums, they are delicious to eat and can also be decoratively wrapped and hung on your Christmas tree or used as stocking stuffers. Stored in an airtight container, your sugarplums will last several months, but only if no one knows where they are!

EQUIPMENT:
Medium-sized mixing bowl
Measuring cups and spoons
Small soup bowl
Medium-sized saucepan
Wooden spoon
Candy thermometer *or* drinking glass
Wax paper
Airtight container
Plastic wrap (optional)

FOODS YOU WILL NEED:
¼ cup candied fruits, citron, *or* orange peel
1½ cups halved *or* broken walnuts, pecans, *or* blanched almonds
2 tablespoons wheat germ
½ cup dried coconut *or* sesame seeds (optional)
⅓ cup orange juice
1 tablespoon grated orange peel
¼ teaspoon orange extract
1½ cups granulated sugar
Ice water

Ingredients:

(To make about 1 pound, or 36 walnut-sized candies)

¼ cup candied fruits, citron, *or* orange peel
1½ cups halved *or* broken walnuts, pecans, *or* blanched almonds
2 tablespoons wheat germ
½ cup granulated sugar *or* dried coconut *or* sesame seeds (optional)

How To:

1. Wash your hands, as you will be molding candies. In mixing bowl, measure and combine candied fruits, nuts, and wheat germ. In small soup bowl, measure out about ½ cup of granulated sugar *or* coconut *or* sesame seeds. Set both bowls aside.

⅓ cup orange juice
1 tablespoon grated orange
 peel
¼ teaspoon orange extract
1 cup granulated sugar

Glass of ice water

2. Measure orange juice, orange peel, orange extract, and sugar into saucepan. Stir with wooden spoon until sugar starts to dissolve.

3. If you have a candy thermometer, clip it to inside of saucepan and tilt it slightly so its tip does not touch bottom of pan.

   Set pan over medium-high heat and cook syrup until thermometer reads 238°, or until a drop of syrup turns into a *soft* ball (see Basic Skills) when spooned into a glass of ice water. Syrup reaches this temperature *very quickly* (approximately 5 minutes, depending upon heat of stove) so watch it carefully and test it often.

4. As soon as syrup is cooked, remove pan from heat. Stir in nut–fruit–wheat germ mixture.

5. Let candy cool 2 or 3 minutes, until it is cool enough to touch, though still warm. With your hands, form candy into walnut-sized balls. Then roll each ball in the bowl of sugar *or* coconut *or* sesame seeds. Set candies on wax paper to cool completely. This step must be done fairly quickly, before candy mixture becomes too cold and stiff to mold. (If it does become too stiff, set pan over hot water for a few minutes.)

ORANGE EPIPHANY CAKE

The twelfth day after Christmas is January 6. This is a special holiday known by three different names: Twelfth Night, Epiphany, and Three Kings' Day. This is said to be the day when the three kings brought gifts to the Christ Child in Bethlehem.

Kings are very important in the celebration of this day. In many European countries, the highlight of Epiphany is the "bean cake," or "King's Cake," served at the end of a festive dinner. A whole bean is hidden in the cake. Whoever receives the portion containing the bean becomes the "king or queen of the bean," receives a crown, a gift, and also good luck in the coming year.

Our recipe is as moist and rich in flavor as any king or queen could wish, has an almond hidden inside, and is baked in a crown-shaped mold.

This cake gets even more delicious the longer it stands, so you can make it a day ahead of time if you like. Keep it wrapped in foil *or* plastic wrap. It also freezes well, wrapped in airtight plastic bag *and/or* foil. Remember to see who gets the bean when the cake is served.

EQUIPMENT:
9″ ring mold (*or* one 8″-square *or* -round layer pan)
Measuring cups and spoons
Wax paper
Electric mixer *or* slotted spoon
Large mixing bowl
Sifter
Rubber scraper
Timer
Cake tester *or* toothpick
Potholders
Table knife
Flat serving platter *or* plate
Foil *or* plastic wrap

FOODS YOU WILL NEED:
1 cup plus 1 tablespoon butter *or* margarine, at room temperature
2 cups plus 6 tablespoons all-purpose flour
1½ cups granulated sugar
¾ cup orange juice plus all grated peel from 2 medium-sized oranges
2 eggs
1 teaspoon orange extract
1 teaspoon baking powder
Pinch of salt
1 whole almond *or* large dry lima bean
Frosting: double Decorative Frosting recipe (see index) *or* confectioners' sugar

Ingredients:	How To:

(To make 9″ ring mold)

1 tablespoon butter *or*
  margarine
3 to 4 tablespoons flour

1. Turn oven on to 350°. Generously grease mold *or* pan with butter. Then sprinkle inside of pan with a little flour. Tip pan over and shake out excess flour onto wax paper. Set pan aside.

1 cup butter *or* margarine,
  at room temperature
1½ cups granulated sugar

2. Use electric mixer *or* spoon to beat butter *or* margarine and sugar together in bowl until smooth and creamy.

2 whole oranges
¾ cup orange juice

3. Grate peel from 2 oranges onto a piece of wax paper. Then squeeze oranges, remove pits, and add more juice if necessary to make ¾ cup. Set juice and peel aside.

2 eggs
1 teaspoon orange extract

4. Break eggs into measuring cup, then add them to butter-sugar mixture in bowl. Add orange juice, orange extract, and orange peel. Beat until smooth. (The curdled look will disappear when flour is added.)

2 cups plus 2 tablespoons
  all-purpose flour
1 teaspoon baking powder
Pinch of salt

5. Sift flour onto wax paper (see Basic Skills), then measure it and add it to other ingredients in bowl. Sift in baking

powder and salt. Beat slowly until well blended. Clean sides of bowl with rubber scraper from time to time.

6. Spoon batter into prepared pan. Empty bowl with rubber scraper. Press 1 almond *or* 1 bean into batter and push it under surface slightly. Smooth top of batter so it is evenly distributed in pan.

BEAN

7. Place cake in preheated oven. Set timer for 55 minutes. When time is up, test with cake tester *or* toothpick. If this comes out clean when stuck into cake, cake is done. If covered with any wet batter, bake cake about 5 minutes longer and test again.

8. Remove cake from oven. Cool about 5 minutes. Then loosen cake by running blade of table knife between cake and pan edges.

9. To unmold cake, set platter *or* plate on top of cake mold. Hold both cake and plate together and turn them upside down. Tap the bottom of the mold lightly with the handle of knife, then lift up mold. Cake should fall gently onto plate.

10. To frost, sift about ⅓ cup confectioners' sugar over cake, until it is lightly covered. Or use double the recipe for Decorative Frosting (see index).

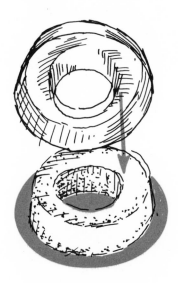

SCANDINAVIAN OAT COOKIES

There is an old Danish saying that all visitors to your house at Christmastime must taste your home-baked cookies. If they neglect to do so, they will "carry off the spirit of Christmas" when they leave. To guard your Christmas spirit, be sure you have enough of these crunchy buttery cookies (known as *Havresmaakager*) to give everyone a sample, in both vanilla and chocolate flavors.

EQUIPMENT:
Small saucepan
Mixing bowls—large and medium-sized
Measuring cups and spoons
Rubber scraper
Electric mixer *or* large spoon
Cookie sheets
2 teaspoons
Timer
Potholders
Spatula *or* pancake turner
Flat platter
Airtight container

FOODS YOU WILL NEED:
1 cup butter
¾ cup granulated sugar
1 egg
1 teaspoon vanilla extract
½ cup all-purpose flour
2 cups rolled oats
½ cup wheat germ
1½ to 4 tablespoons unsweetened
 powdered cocoa (optional)

Ingredients:

How To:

(To make about 60 cookies)

1 cup (2 sticks) butter

¾ cup granulated sugar

1. Wash your hands. Turn on oven to 350°.

2. Measure butter into saucepan and set it over low heat on stove. When butter melts, remove pan from stove and turn off heat. Set pan aside so butter can cool.

3. While butter is melting, measure ¾ cup sugar into large bowl. Pour melted and cooled butter over sugar. Empty butter pan with rubber scraper. Use electric mixer *or* spoon to beat mixture well.

1 egg
1 teaspoon vanilla extract
½ cup all-purpose flour
2 cups rolled oats
½ cup wheat germ

1½ to 2 tablespoons un-
    sweetened powdered cocoa
    (optional)

BATTER WILL BE QUITE SOFT.

4. Break egg into measuring cup. Then add egg to ingredients in bowl. Add vanilla and beat. Add flour, oats, and wheat germ. Use electric mixer *or* spoon to blend everything together very well.

5. If you want to make half the cookies chocolate-flavored, place half the dough in the medium-sized bowl. Add cocoa and blend well. (To make entire recipe chocolate, add 3 to 4 tablespoons cocoa in step 4.)

6. Scoop a lump of dough into one teaspoon and push it off onto the *ungreased* cookie sheet with the second tea-spoon *or* your finger. Set cookies about 1½″ apart.

7. Place cookie sheet in 350° oven and set timer to bake for 10 to 12 minutes, *or* until a dark golden edge forms around cookies.

8. Remove pans from oven with potholders. Leave cookies on sheet until they are completely cold and hard (when hot, they will be too soft to pick up). Use spatula *or* pancake turner to transfer cold cookies to platter.

GINGERBREAD MEN AND WOMEN

In Sweden, these traditional Christmas cookies are also shaped like pigs, horses, and roosters. Decorate your cookies with raisins or the icing recipe that follows. Hang the cookies on your tree. Or pack up a basket of different shapes and give them as a gift. NOTE: You can make your own patterns by copying and enlarging our designs. Cut your shapes from flexible cardboard. Lightly flour your pattern, set it on the rolled dough, and trace around the edges with a toothpick. Remove the pattern and cut the cookie out with the floured tip of a knife.

EQUIPMENT:
Cookie sheet
Sifter
Wax paper
Measuring cups and spoons
3 mixing bowls—small, medium, and
    large
3 teacups
Electric mixer *or* slotted spoon
Rubber scraper
Large spoon
Rolling pin
Cookie cutters *or* cardboard patterns
    and paring knife
Toothpick
Timer
Spatula
Wire rack (optional)
Decorating tube (see General Equip-
    ment List)
Christmas tree hanging ribbons
    (optional; 12″ lengths of ¼″-wide
    ribbon)
Paring knife
Lemon *or* orange juice squeezer
    (optional)
Strainer
Dishtowel *or* plastic wrap

FOODS YOU WILL NEED:
½ cup plus 2 tablespoons butter
    or margarine
3⅓ cups all-purpose flour
½ teaspoon salt
½ teaspoon baking soda
1 teaspoon ground cloves
1 teaspoon cinnamon
½ teaspoon ground nutmeg
2½ teaspoons ground ginger
½ teaspoon ground cardamom
½ cup dark brown sugar
½ cup molasses, preferably
    unsulfured type
1 egg
Seedless raisins (optional)

For Royal Icing:
2 tablespoons lemon juice
2 egg whites
⅛ teaspoon cream of tartar
⅛ teaspoon salt
3½ cups confectioners' sugar

(86)

Ingredients:

(To make about 30 figures 5″ tall)

1 to 2 tablespoons butter *or* margarine

3⅓ cups all-purpose flour
½ teaspoon salt
½ teaspoon baking soda
1 teaspoon ground cloves
1 teaspoon cinnamon
½ teaspoon ground nutmeg
2½ teaspoons ground ginger
½ teaspoon ground cardamom

½ cup butter *or* margarine
½ cup firmly packed dark brown sugar
½ cup molasses

1 egg

How To:

1. Turn oven on to 350°.

2. Grease cookie sheet lightly with butter *or* margarine.

3. Sift flour onto wax paper. Then measure 3 cups of flour into medium-sized bowl. Set aside extra flour. Add salt, baking soda, and spices.

4. In largest bowl, add butter *or* margarine, sugar (packed down well in measuring cup), and molasses.

5. Break egg into cup, then add it to butter-sugar-molasses mixture in bowl. Beat with slotted spoon *or* electric mixer (on medium speed) until smooth and creamy. Clean sides of bowl with rubber scraper.

(87)

6. Spoon flour mixture a little at a time into butter-sugar-egg mixture. Beat slowly until all flour is added and dough forms a stiff ball. If dough still feels sticky, add more flour from the extra amount set aside. Add flour 1 tablespoonful at a time until dough is dry enough to handle easily.

7. Take about ⅓ of dough and roll it out to between ⅛" and ¼" thick on lightly floured pastry board or between 2 pieces of wax paper (see Basic Skills).

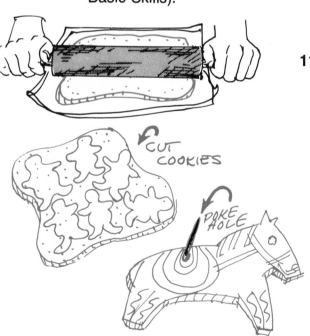

CUT COOKIES

POKE HOLE

8. Wrap remaining dough in wax paper and chill it in refrigerator until needed to make additional batches of cookies.

9. Dip cookie cutters in flour (or cut around patterns as directed in the beginning of the recipe). Shake cutters to remove excess flour, then cut cookies as shown. Peel away extra dough between shapes, then use lightly floured spatula to lift cookies. Place them about 1" away from each other on greased sheet. Press raisin eyes, nose, mouth, and buttons into cookies if you wish (or decorate them later with icing).

10. Use toothpick to poke ⅛"-diameter hole in each cookie you want to hang on the tree.

11. Set timer to bake 8 to 12 minutes, or until cookies are firm and a *slightly* darker color around edges. Use spatula to remove warm cookies from cookie sheet; cool them flat on wire rack *or* on wax paper. When cookies are cold, they can be decorated with Royal Icing.

ROYAL ICING

This icing becomes very hard and is good to use when trimming cookies that will be exposed to the air when they are hung on the Christmas tree. If you want to tint icing, add a few drops of vegetable food coloring.

Ingredients:

(To make about 2 cups of icing)

Juice of 1 lemon (about 2
   tablespoons)

2 egg whites

⅛ teaspoon cream of tartar
⅛ teaspoon salt
3½ cups confectioners'
   sugar, approximately

How To:

1. Cut and squeeze lemon; strain lemon juice into a cup and set it aside.

2. Separate eggs (see Basic Skills). Set aside yolks in a cup for another use. Put whites in mixing bowl. With electric mixer *or* eggbeater, beat whites until slightly foamy.

3. Mix cream of tartar and salt into beaten egg whites. Sift measured sugar—½ cup at a time—directly into the same bowl. Beat mixture after each addition of sugar. Stir in lemon juice until icing reaches correct consistency; it should be like softly whipped cream. Sift in a little more sugar if icing is too thin.

4. To keep icing from hardening, keep bowl covered with damp (not wet) dishtowel *or* plastic wrap. Place icing in decorating tube and add decorations to cooled cookies. Tie ribbons through cookies that will hang on tree.

ROLLED SUGAR COOKIES

Star-shaped, tree-shaped, Santa-shaped cookies—gaily frosted and sparkling on a platter . . . that is what Christmas cooking is really all about! Certainly, without these cookies, it just would not seem like Christmas.

Nothing is more fun than getting together with a group of friends or family shortly before the holiday to mix, roll, cut, and decorate these old favorites. The only difficulty is in saving any of the cookies until Christmas. Better be safe and make several batches, as well as several of the differently shaped variations that follow the recipe. NOTE: Frosting recipe follows the cookies.

EQUIPMENT:
Cookie sheets
Mixing cups and spoons
Electric mixer *or* slotted spoon
Mixing bowls—large and medium-sized
Sifter
Wax paper
Large spoon
Rolling pin
Pastry board (optional)
Cookie cutters
Spatula *or* pancake turner
Toothpick
Timer
Potholders
Wire rack
Large flat tray
Double boiler (optional)
Plastic bag *or* aluminum foil (optional)
Airtight container *or* cookie jar

FOODS YOU WILL NEED:
About 1 cup butter *or* margarine, at
    room temperature
1 cup granulated sugar
2 *or* 3 eggs
1 teaspoon vanilla *or* almond extract
2¾ to 3 cups all-purpose flour
1 teaspoon baking powder
1 teaspoon salt

Optional flavorings
Granulated sugar *or* finely
    chopped nuts
2 tablespoons powdered cocoa *or*
    1 square (1 ounce) Baker's
    chocolate
Marzipan (see index)
Vegetable food coloring

Ingredients:

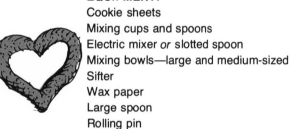

(To make about 48 cookies)

2 tablespoons butter *or*
    margarine

¾ cup butter *or* margarine,
    at room temperature
1 cup granulated sugar

How To:

1. Turn oven on to 350°. Wash your hands. Grease cookie sheets with butter *or* margarine and set them aside.

2. Use electric mixer *or* slotted spoon to beat together butter and sugar in large bowl.

2 eggs
1 teaspoon vanilla *or* almond
   extract

2¾ to 3 cups all-purpose
   flour
1 teaspoon baking powder
1 teaspoon salt

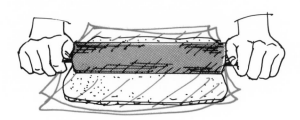

3. Break eggs into measuring cup, then add them to butter-sugar mixture. Add vanilla *or* almond extract and beat well.

4. Sift 3 cups flour onto wax paper. Then measure 2¾ cups of it into medium-sized bowl. Sift baking powder and salt over flour in bowl.

5. Spoon about half the bowl of flour mixture into egg-butter mixture and beat slowly until blended. Add remaining flour mixture and beat. Dough should form a ball and feel quite dry though pliable, like soft clay or a pie-crust dough. If dough seems too soft, add more flour—1 tablespoon at a time—from wax paper.

6. When dough is correct consistency, roll out about ⅓ of dough on lightly floured pastry board *or* between 2 floured sheets of wax paper (see Basic Skills). Roll dough between ⅛″ and ¼″ thick.

7. Wrap remaining dough in wax paper and chill it in the refrigerator until needed to make additional batches of cookies.

8. Dip cookie cutters in flour. Shake cutters to remove excess flour, then cut cookies as shown. Peel away extra dough between shapes, then use lightly floured spatula *or* pancake turner to lift cookies and place them about 1″ away from each other on greased cookie sheets.

9. Use toothpick to poke ⅛″-diameter hole in any cookies you will want to hang on your Christmas tree.

10. If you do not wish to frost cookies, they can now be brushed with beaten whole egg—or egg white—and sprinkled with finely chopped nuts *or* granulated sugar.

11. Place cookies in 350° oven. Set timer for 8 to 12 minutes. Bake until cookies are golden at the edges. Remove pan with potholders and turn off oven. Let cookies cool a couple of minutes, then use spatula to remove them from sheet. Cool cookies on wire rack. When cookies are cold, you can decorate them.

VARIATIONS
(All are baked at 350° for 10 to 12 minutes or until just golden):

Chocolate Spirals

1. Make Rolled Sugar Cookies, steps 1 to 5. Divide dough in half. Set half on wax paper. Add 2 tablespoons unsweetened cocoa *or* 1 square melted Baker's chocolate to dough in bowl. (To melt Baker's chocolate, see French Chocolate Truffle recipe, step 3.) Use your hands or a spoon to blend chocolate into dough.

2. Flour your hands. On lightly floured pastry board *or* wax paper, roll chocolate dough into a fat cylinder roughly 6″ or 7″ x 1½″, as shown. Make a cylinder the same size out of the plain dough.

NOTE: Marzipan (see index) may be used in place of chocolate dough.

3. On lightly floured pastry board *or* between 2 lightly floured sheets of wax paper (see Basic Skills), roll out each cylinder—1 at a time—into a long rectangle about 7″ x 14″ and ⅛″ thick.

4. Set strip of chocolate dough on top of plain dough. To pick it up easily, use a floured spatula *or*—if rolled on wax paper—pick paper up and turn it upside down.

5. Roll the 2 layers together like a jelly roll as shown. Wrap the roll in wax paper and chill for about an hour *or* longer. (Dough may also be frozen at this point, wrapped in airtight plastic bag *or* foil.)

6. To bake, cut ¼″ slices off roll and place on greased cookie sheets. Do not frost spirals.

Wreaths, Pretzels, and Hearts

1. Make Rolled Sugar Cookies, steps 1 to 5. Divide dough in half, or in smaller divisions.

2. Color 1 piece of dough with several drops of vegetable food coloring *or* 1 *or* 2 tablespoons of cocoa, kneaded in.

3. Flour hands. Between your palms, roll 1″ balls of colored dough and 1″ balls of white dough. Roll each ball into a rope about ½″ x 7″.

4. To make wreaths, set 2 differently colored dough ropes side by side and pinch them together at one end. Twist ropes over each other, then form into a circle. Pinch ends to hold. Tie single ropes into loose knots to make pretzels, or bend into heart shapes. Set on greased cookie sheets.

5. Brush cookies with beaten egg *or* egg white. Sprinkle them with granulated sugar *or* finely chopped nuts.

Candy Canes

1. Same as Wreath, *except* in step 3, roll balls a little smaller than 1″; roll balls into ropes about ⅜″ x 6″.

2. Set 2 differently colored ropes side by side, pinch to hold them at one end, then twist ropes over and over. Pinch other ends to hold.

3. Set twists on greased cookie sheet. Bend top 2″ of each cookie over into a curve with the tip about 1″ away from straight part of cane.

DECORATIVE FROSTING

EQUIPMENT:
Small saucepan
Mixing bowl
Rubber scraper
Measuring cups and spoons
Sifter
Large spoon, teaspoon
Custard cups *or* teacups—1 for each
    color you will tint frosting
Decorating tube(s) (see General Equip-
    ment List) *or* butter knives (to spread
    frosting)

FOODS YOU WILL NEED:
2 tablespoons butter *or* margarine
2 cups confectioners' sugar
1 teaspoon vanilla extract *or* strained
    lemon juice
2 *or* 3 tablespoons milk *or* light cream
Vegetable food coloring *and/or* seedless
    raspberry jam *or* beet juice instead
    of red coloring

Ingredients:

(To make about ¾ cup)

2 tablespoons butter *or*
   margarine
2 cups confectioners' sugar
1 teaspoon vanilla extract *or*
   strained lemon juice
2 *or* 3 tablespoons milk *or*
   light cream

Vegetable food coloring *and/or*
seedless raspberry jam *or*
beet juice for red color

How To:

1. Place butter *or* margarine in
small saucepan and set over
low heat until melted. Remove
from heat and set aside.

2. Sift sugar into bowl. Add
melted butter, cleaning pan
with rubber scraper. Add
vanilla *or* lemon juice and milk
or cream. Beat until smooth.

3. Frosting should be of a consistency that will spread easily.
If it feels too stiff, add more
milk *or* cream, 1 teaspoon at
a time. If it feels too soft, sift
in a little more sugar.

4. Place a couple of tablespoons
of frosting in each cup. Blend
in a few drops of coloring.

5. Spread frosting on cookies
with butter knives *or* put frosting in decorating tube and
squeeze out fancy trimmings.

WASSAIL CHRISTMAS PUNCH

Both the recipe and the word *wassail* come to us from the British Isles, where wassail has been popular for centuries. In Old English, *waes hael* means "to your health," and from this toast came the name of the drink, made from hot-spiced fruit juice. In medieval times, the wassail was used to tell fortunes on New Year's Eve. A ring or piece of fruit was dropped into the wassail bowl. The person who scooped the token into a punch cup would marry during the coming year. Tell your own fortunes with orange slices in the wassail.

EQUIPMENT:
Toothpick
Measuring cups and spoons
Large pot *or* Dutch oven
Ladle
Punch cups *or* mugs

FOODS YOU WILL NEED:
1 whole lemon *or* orange

1 box whole cloves
½ gallon apple cider
½ gallon cranberry juice
½ to 1 cup dark *or* light brown sugar
2 teaspoons cinnamon
1 teaspoon ground ginger
½ teaspoon ground allspice
1 teaspoon ground cloves
Cinnamon sticks (optional)

Ingredients:

(To make 32 ½-cup servings)
1 whole lemon *or* orange
1 box whole cloves
½ gallon apple cider
½ gallon cranberry juice (*or* 1 gallon of either juice alone)
½ to 1 cup dark *or* light brown sugar (sweeten to taste)
2 teaspoons cinnamon
1 teaspoon ground ginger
½ teaspoon ground allspice
1 teaspoon ground cloves
Cinnamon sticks (optional)

How To:

1. Use toothpick to poke holes close together all over a lemon *or* orange. Stick a clove in each hole.

2. Place cider, juice, sugar, spices (except cinnamon stick), and clove-studded fruit in large pot. Set it on stove over medium heat and bring almost to a boil.

3. Turn heat down to low and simmer punch about 30 minutes. Turn off heat. Let punch cool slightly if too hot. Ladle warm punch directly into cups *or* mugs. A whole cinnamon stick can be added to each cup for a stirrer.

 # *Index*